Adjusted Sails

Adjusted Sails

What Does This Make Possible?

Kathi C. Laughman

mackenzie
circle

ISBN: 0998274305
ISBN 9780998274300
Library of Congress Control Number: 2017903094
The Mackenzie Circle LLC, Spring, TEXAS

Published by The Mackenzie Circle LLC, Spring, Texas.

Printed in the United States of America

Dedication

To my parents, Earl and Peggy Cooper

*Thank you for your unwavering belief
in the miracle of my possibilities.*

"It is the set of the sails, not the direction of the wind that determines which way we will go.

You must take personal responsibility. You can't change the circumstances, the seasons, or the wind, but you can change yourself. That is something you have charge of."

Jim Rohn

"For I know the plans I have for you," declares the Lord, "Plans to prosper you and not to harm you, plans to give you hope and a future."
Jeremiah 29:11

Contents

Author's Note

**Sometimes in the winds of change,
we find our true direction.**

Have you ever started doing one thing and it morphed into something else? Something completely different? When I started writing this book, it was about something else. That's probably why it never got finished. It wasn't the right book. I developed outlines—many in fact. I wrote quite a few words. But the book stayed just inside the edges of done.

The book began to feel a bit like a metaphor for where I was in my life. There was something more there; I could sense it. Some days I could even see it. But my direction wasn't certain. I told a friend that at times the picture of what was next for me was so clear it was like a haunting. Haunting because it seemed that if I reached for it too quickly or vigorously, it would be like disturbing the surface of water. The vision would be lost.

I think most of us are fine when we know what we're up against. When I have data that I can transform into information,

I'm a master at envisioning the way through. It's when there is missing information and I'm operating without knowing what might be coming that my performance can falter, even fail.

Fear of the unknown. The winds of change.

Living with uncertainty is hard. How do you prepare for what's next when you don't have a clue what's coming? And today, what is certain is that we face universal and, what seemingly is all encompassing, uncertainty. There is a military term that I believe is a perfect descriptor for our world today. It is VUCA: an acronym for Volatility, Uncertainty, Chaos, and Ambiguity.

I have come to understand that the secret to living a fulfilled life, even in this VUCA world we live in, is simple. It is found in our resiliency muscle.

The idea that someone else is more adept or charmed than anyone else for facing what life brings is false. We each have it within our power to thrive regardless of what we may encounter or even cause in life.

Most abilities, including resiliency, owe their existence to skill versus talent, something that can be learned and mastered. And that is what this book is ultimately about—the power and value of the skill of resiliency.

Why is it important for me to share this with you? The answer is simple. Because resiliency has proven to be the most effective changemaker for good in my own life. It is ultimately what led me to a joy I had never known, a joy that has remained. From there, sharing the experience to serve others is a natural part of the cycle, even a responsibility.

Travel back with me to a cold November night, not so many years past. My life was about to take several drastic and unexpected turns. That's not to say I hadn't gone through transitions, even significant disruptions before. There had been many singular events to absorb.

But this time, they kept coming, like multiple waves on a beach that became more and more deserted. With each wave, I experienced a completely different level and source of challenge.

Has that happened to you? You believe you've met a problem head-on only to find there was another one lurking just beyond the corner. And then another.

That November, after living for more than two decades as a single parent, in a shower of rice at my daughter's wedding, my personal status moved from single Mom to single Empty Nester. I had just turned 50.

It seemed a natural progression of life events, but it held far more significance than I had imagined. I had great plans, but I was not prepared for the emotional aftermath. Without my child, who would need me now?

A short while later, my professional life was changed by a pink slip. I left the halls of the executive suites to join the throngs of the unemployed in tough economic times. Overnight my identity was again in crisis. Without my work, who was I?

Keeping pace, my world shifted again while sitting in a doctor's office. My health was demanding immediate and total attention. A tough, year-long battle with Hepatitis C brought me to my knees. Without my health, what kind of future was I facing?

Empty nest. Empty job. Empty health. Empty.

Just as I began to regain my footing after each disruption, the next seemingly random act of life appeared. Not exactly what I had envisioned or planned, especially at midlife where things were supposed to be coming together and the years of sacrifice were supposed to be producing a payoff. I can tell you that this did not feel like a payoff. It felt like a payback. But for what? Initially, it all felt immensely unfair.

In those moments, my resiliency was put to the test. Those times were not easy. There were long days and even longer nights. There were fears and many tears. At each juncture, I had to choose between being diminished or being increased by what was happening in my life.

We meet ourselves in the most intimate way in these moments. Because change is hard, especially when you liked things the way they were!

I had to learn to recognize the difference between something happening *to* me versus something happening *for* or *through* me. That is one of the keys to discovering the true source of personal power in resilience. That was without question the initial shift for me—the growth from *Why me?* to *Why not me?* as a leading-edge question.

I respect that pain is personal. There is truly no competition in grief. I am certain that others have experienced far more tragic events than these. But after listening to countless stories of others, I also know that there is a universal thread connecting us through our experiences with pain and loss, even if the specific plot twists are different.

What I learned was that even though each wave brought significant loss, it also brought something new. My life was becoming richer, fuller. Not diminished. That's the real story. It's not about what I went through. It is about the possibilities that were born from what initially only felt like loss. I had a clear realization that it isn't about what happens to us. It is about what *we create* from what happens to us. That is how we embark on and continue our journey with unshakable joy.

My hope is that my experiences and the lessons from this season in my life will also speak to what you need. Perhaps like me, you can discover a new perspective that allows you to embrace with gratitude and joy whatever your life brings.

The winds will blow. But you can adjust your sails.

How is that possible? It will not come from simply reading. It will require you to rewrite the lessons into your own life. I can deliver the message, but in the end, you must live it for yourself. And then, my friend, the torch will be passed. It will be your turn to lead.

Are you ready to adjust your sails? Let's get started.

Start at the Bottom: Getting the Foundation Right

Do you wish to rise? Begin by descending.
You plan a tower that will pierce the clouds?
Lay first the foundation of humility.
~SAINT AUGUSTINE

After many years of living in places owned by other people, I felt a special pride at the title company's office when I was handed the keys to my own home.

Because I was the original owner, I had the privilege of working with the builder and watching the house go from blueprint to punch list.

There were many life lessons during that process, but none more profound than those around the importance of having a sound and well-thought-out foundation. Everything about the house's possibilities started there.

I remember going to the property soon after the concrete slab had been poured. My daughter Lauren and I walked around imagining walls and windows. Standing there on that foundation, we were creating a vision for our life. It gave shape to everything to come as our future home rose from the ground to its completion.

Each time we visited, we saw progress. Everything was changing except one thing: that foundation. It kept everything aligned and moving toward the finished vision.

Resiliency begins in that same place. Our personal foundation is what gives shape to everything that will come. Everything in our personal vision relies on us having a foundation that can support bringing it to fruition. Nothing is more fundamental as we move forward than having a foundation that supports us on the journey.

When the foundation is right, the house of our life will stand. The structural support is built on the solid footing of that core design. It will need maintenance and care, even some significant attention over time, but to stand, it begins with the right foundation.

The achievable impact of our resilience will depend on the foundation we use to build our lives. It is what is needed before all else.

Let's examine then what resilience is about and why that foundation and vision are so critical. Resiliency is often misunderstood. We tend to think of it as enduring a drudgery or hardship. But that is not its true profile. Resiliency isn't about martyrdom or endurance. It is not about getting through something. It is profoundly more.

Resilience is about overcoming, transforming, innovating. In short, it's the true genesis for living a fulfilled, enriched, and joy-filled life. When we are resilient, we take what happens and USE it. We create from it. We don't simply endure. We transform our lives by defining the purpose of our experiences as something that serves us and what we value.

We often hear that it's not what happens to you, it's how you react or respond to it. We spout those words without a true understanding of what they mean. We stop short of defining what is indeed at stake and what we can do.

The first part of the statement is true—it is not about what happens to us. It is the second part that needs work. Our reaction is going to be based on our perception of what happens to us. It stems from the value and meaning we give it and what we do with it.

That is the essence of resilience. If we want to change our reaction, we must change our perspective, even our philosophical point of view of what crosses our life path. That is the beginning of the foundation.

It is not about what happens to us. It is about what we *CREATE* from what happens to us. It is about how we leverage everything that happens in our lives to achieve something that matters. That is resilience.

Chapter 1

Unlocking the Code:
There Is No Hidden Secret

*D*o you ever wonder why some people seem to have a deeper capacity for absorbing life's rhythm? No matter what happens, they seem to land on their feet, ready to go without missing a step. Is it how they are wired? Is there a *resiliency* gene that some of us get but is missing for the rest of us?

From time to time, I volunteer to work on the inner circle launch teams for books being published that I believe are going to have significant impact. It's a labor of love as an author myself, but it's also a way to be a part of something meaningful.

Such was the case when I heard about Jen Bricker's book *Everything is Possible*.[1] Jen is the ultimate inspiration when it comes to defying the odds. There is a line from Shakespeare's *A Midsummer Night's Dream* that says, "Though she be but little, she is fierce!" I had those words inscribed on a plaque

---

1 Bricker, Jen (2016). *Everything is Possible: Finding the Faith and Courage to Follow Your Dreams*. Grand Rapids, MI: Baker Publishing Group.

for my second grand-girl, and it was no surprise to me that it also showed up in the introduction to Jen's book.

In case you're not familiar with her story, Jen was born without legs. Her biological parents did not think they could care for her and gave her up for adoption. Let that sink in for a moment. It doesn't sound like a promising start. Her adoptive parents, though, had no fear at all. They taught her to "Never say can't." Imagine!

Because she adopted that mantra, today she is a champion tumbler, aerial artist, author, and speaker. She inspires thousands with her can-do message. Here is her perspective shared in the book: "If an obstacle presented itself, I got creative and figured out how to get around it. It's an attitude that I feel people aren't taught, which is probably why I get asked for advice all the time. Life is an amazing journey if you're not afraid to live it."

My dear friend and fellow author Justina Page is another example of living resilience. In her book, *The Circle of Fire: In the Midst of the Ashes an Ember of Hope Flickered*[2], she tells her family's story. A four-alarm house fire was a devastating and life-altering tragedy. The loss of their home, severe injuries, and the death of one of their precious children.

Much healing had already happened by the time I met Justina. She had accomplished so much. A writer, playwright, lyricist — even now working on a movie production. It was painful for me to read her book, and yet I knew that to honor

---

2 Page, Justina (2015). *The Circle of Fire: In the Midst of the Ashes an Ember of Hope Flickered*. New York, NY: Morgan James Publishing.

her journey, I needed to know more about that path. It broke my heart to travel back through her writing to those dark and painful days, but it lifted my spirit in a way not many books can or do because I know the story is still being written. And it is a beautiful story.

In chapter 18 of her book, she shares this very personal wisdom: "I had stumbled upon purpose. Purpose is powerful. It is the warring faction that combats the 'why me' syndrome. It disarms and conquers confusion every time. When you know what you are destined for, you can get to the business of making it happen."

There are stories after stories about amazing people, like Jen and Justina. Beating all the odds and overcoming incredible obstacles.

What does it take for them to write that story with their life? We stand in awe. We cannot imagine that being within our power to emulate. Why is that? I believe in part it is because we think that there is a secret that is only revealed to some. We see it as a strength you are born with, or not. And we fear we are in the "or not" category.

Just how much faith do we have? Could you pray: "God, surprise me!" without fear? That was the challenge put to me not long ago. True confession: The thought gave me pause.

But then I remembered. It was in the surprises that I had found my deepest joy. It was in the unsettling that I found my center. It was in the wondering that I had found that the secret wasn't an answer. It was a question. The answer is a question that has manifested throughout history and is the first step in mastering resilience.

The question is this: *What does this make possible?*

In its simplest form, those five words define resilience. What does this make possible?

Some of my favorite television shows are cooking competitions. They usually involve these elements: 1) A common ingredient or ingredients; 2) A stocked pantry; 3) A limited amount of time; 4) The contestants' own unique experience as a chef; and 5) Their ability to think creatively, to be resilient!

The criteria to win the competition are exacting. All the specified ingredients must be used. But beyond that, they must be identifiable AND transformed. That's not an easy thing to pull off. The challenge? Take this vegetable and transform it, but make sure I can still tell it's this vegetable when I taste it.

Each contestant gets the same ingredients, has access to the same pantry, and faces the same clock counting down second by second. But they don't all excel. Some forget an ingredient. Some do not transform it. Some transform it beyond recognition or haven't really leveraged its attributes in a meaningful way.

But some—ah, the geniuses that are masters—are resilient from the moment they open their basket. When they look inside, they ask this question: What does this make possible?

Life works the same way. We're all given certain things that are essentially the same. We all have access to the same or at least similar resources. And we know that time remains the equalizer of us all. It is for those among us able to ask that question each day when we open the baskets of our lives that true success and achievement is possible. Because we ask the question: What does THIS make possible?

You may think that this isn't plausible in every situation. You may feel like life has dealt you a hand that leaves you at a disadvantage. Jen, Justina, and I would dare to disagree.

The wisdom of the ages tells us that success and achievement is possible, even in your situation, whatever that may be. You may think this sounds somewhat exploitive. Perhaps it is, but in a productive way that is ultimately for good. You may think that when we encounter absolute heartbreak that this is the last thing we think about. Yet, it still serves.

As I shared in the introduction, I faced some tough life shifts in succession all within a compressed time span. But in each case, my forward momentum came when I could honestly ask this question: What does this make possible?

When I became an empty nester, possibilities appeared that were not there when I had the primary day-to-day responsibility for another life.

When I found myself unemployed, I was propelled into a place where the options were vast. I would not have even considered them had my professional world not stopped spinning for that moment.

When I heard the words "What do you know about Hepatitis C?" it was without question the toughest time for resilience. So, of course, it was where it was most needed. But even there, my recovery could not begin until the question was asked so the answers could begin to appear.

Life happens. It's a challenge for all of us at some point. How can we be prepared to cope, to be resilient and create meaning? You see, there is the magic, the ancient wisdom. Let's revisit this for a moment. It is not about what happens to us. It is not about what is in the basket. It is about what we create from it. Do you see the distinction? Not how we react, what we create.

To be prepared for life, to get to this place of resiliency, just like those chefs, we must continuously develop our personal best. We do this through practicing life skills that drive change within us that will also grow our interactions and influence in the world in a meaningful way.

When we focus on mastering life skills, we intuitively adopt life practices that allow us to cope with disruptions and detours. We keep building on that foundation for resilience and, ultimately, personal success and significance.

Once you begin working on knowing yourself at the deepest level and how you respond and assimilate your experiences into your personal philosophy, it becomes second nature to check yourself. Resilience is served.

Begin right now with any changes that happen in your day. A meeting cancels. Ask yourself: "What does that makes possible?" Your child is ill, and you must juggle schedules. Ask what that makes possible? You burn dinner. What does that make possible?

When Denis Waitley, performance coach and author of *The Psychology of Winning*[3], worked with world-class athletes

---

3 Waitley, Denis. (1986). *The Psychology of Winning: Ten Qualities of a Total Winner*. New York, NY: Penguin Random House.

competing in the Olympics, he coached them to see their performance as an extension of their daily drills. In fact, the words they spoke to themselves as they would take to the court or track were these: Just like drill.

For every moment when there is a change in plan, ask the question. Before you know it, you'll be moving into action even without thought. It becomes a natural, engrained response. The essence of resilience becomes an organic part of who you are and how you live. Just like drill.

Think about these words from one of the great masters, Pablo Picasso: "There are painters who transform the sun to a yellow spot, but there are others who with the help of their art and their intelligence, transform a yellow spot into sun."

What suns will you create?

Chapter 2

Why Not Me?
A Question of Perspective

*T*here is a statement used within personal development discussions that asserts that how we do *anything* is how we do *everything*. For example, if you lack personal discipline in one area (e.g., health), odds are high that you lack personal discipline in other areas (finance, family commitments, etc.) If you do things in a mediocre way in one area, chances are you look for the easy way out in other areas.

Initially, I struggled with this concept because I believed that I was in fact different in my performance in certain areas of my life. Perhaps you have struggled with this as well. I could see a variance between my discipline in my professional practices versus personal. Then I realized that, at a minimum, how we do anything will certainly affect or impact how we do everything. And that was enough to garner my attention.

Considering that concept, our personal value system starts with our beliefs about ourselves, and that is going to work like an automated GPS, directing our steps. What we have inputted into that GPS is going to affect the output. And that is going to affect everything, especially where we are going.

This is noticeably relevant when we talk about resilience because we all have an internal response mechanism based on certain triggers. There is a question that I believe demonstrates this very clearly and is another word picture for resilience. It is this: *Why not me?*

Most of us have experienced a *Why me?* moment or two. When we move into resilience as a life practice skill, we add the word 'not' that completely alters the question. It's an important word. It acts like a knot. It ties together *why* and *me*. It sends us in search of the why FOR me instead of the why TO me.

The remarkable part is that even this question becomes a learned response—you don't have to be born with this outlook. Asking *Why not me?* won't just be about the challenge; it will also be about the quest. It isn't just *Why not me to lose my job?* It's also *Why not me to start my own company, to get the promotion, to achieve optimal health?* It works as a positioning statement instead of a victim statement.

This helps us rethink all the preconceived limitations that we may have believed restricted our possibilities. It's a healthy exercise to ask ourselves this question and be completely honest with ourselves in our response.

We may have to back into the question, though, to really grasp the concept. Sometimes the first answer is our path to a deeper one.

For many years, I thought I was too much *this* or not enough *that*. Those were the surface answers to my initial *Why not me?* question. I didn't see it as exploratory, but rather a way to find the excuse.

For the question to be effective, it should move to a higher plane. It must become a challenge, even a mantra. *Why not me?*

To be clear, it must be exploratory in a way that allows us to recognize valid reasons why something is outside of our reach at any given time. In those cases, the answers can become the road map to changing the result.

We must first give ourselves permission to ask the question so that we can create a healthier and more valid perspective. From that perspective, we are then able to fully see the possibilities.

In high school, music was a core part of my life. I was vocally talented, and my piano was a favored friend. I learned to read music before I learned to read books. Even though there was invested practice for the skill, what was most encompassing was the fact that I just loved music. I was happiest within the clouds and textures of melodic sound. Because of that, it was a natural conclusion that as I moved on past high school, music would be my field of choice. And at first it was.

To financially afford a college education, I competed in various contests and ultimately won a scholarship to a private college. I found myself hundreds of miles away from home on what initially felt like a grand adventure. What I discovered in the reality was that as much as I loved music, it wasn't what I wanted as my work. In the end, I left college disillusioned and without a degree.

Over the course of my professional life, there were many situations where I felt that the missing college degree was a detriment. There were opportunities that I did not even aspire to because I didn't meet that stated qualification. This became almost an obsession for me later in my career, even after I had attained success. Imposter syndrome was alive and well and, no matter how unwarranted, quite real.

When I asked the question *Why not me?* around some specific career opportunities, the answer always came back that I did not have a degree. But that was just the first part. When I asked what actions I should take, I recognized that I *could change the answer*. I could change the answer by getting the degree. That became my road map.

Once again, I found myself enrolled in college; only this time, there was no scholarship. I was a working business leader and full-time college student. The first semester was brutal as I got my legs under me for handling the dual responsibilities of work and school. But then it became purposeful. I was closing a gap I had regretted for decades. More than that, I was having a great time doing it. Since learning is a core value and passion for me, it was like getting a new source of oxygen. It was a treasured experience and an accomplishment I continue to appreciate.

When we ask the *Why not me?* question and an action response is not clear, that is when we need to practice what I call resilience research. Whatever the initial response, research and find others who faced the same situation, had the same vision, and achieved it.

Those stories are out there. They are just waiting for us to find them so that they can shine the light on our own paths. Quite often, it isn't enough to just have platitudes saying we can achieve our dream and to just keep believing. There is real value in finding others that have been where we are and achieved the success we envision as a point of inspiration.

In the words of Sir Isaac Newton: "If I have seen further, it is by standing on the shoulders of giants."

Why not me? Of course, it's me! How clear it is now.

Chapter 3

What We Accept as True, We Do: The Impact of Belief

*Y*our beliefs are like a lens. They go beyond any technology man has ever developed. Your belief lens filters out, distorts, softens, and expands. For us to empower our full potential, it is paramount that we understand and take responsibility for our beliefs.

In the words of Henry David Thoreau: "It doesn't matter what you look at. It matters what you see." Your beliefs create your vision. They determine what you see. What you believe.

There is a popular graphic that demonstrates this well. Imagine that there is a large number 6 on a card lying on a desk with two people, one on each side of the desk. They are both looking at the same card. On one side, the person will clearly see the number 6 and believe with absolute certainty that is what the card represents.

But on the other side of the desk, that person will say with just as much certainty that it is not a 6, but a 9. Their positioning is like our belief systems. It is our point of view. Depending on what side of the number you're on, your belief shifts. It doesn't matter that you are both looking at the same card; it matters what each of you sees.

Have you ever had to do something you did not want to do? Have you ever had to make a choice you knew was the right decision but was not an easy pact to make with yourself? We are faced with the power of our beliefs when we face decisions that take us to an uncomfortable place. What we *want* and what we *believe* are often in conflict.

Sometimes we refer to beliefs as mindset. While they are separate, they are intertwined to the extent that a differentiation can be hard to make.

Think of it as a progression:

- Beliefs create our mindset.
- Mindset creates our patterns of thinking.
- Those thought patterns create our actions.
- From our actions, we get our results.

That may sound complex and it can be, but it is split-second conditioning that we rarely examine. And we should.

To change a belief means we must make a new decision. To do that, we need to look at why we believe something. There are many reasons. It can have its genesis in a personal experience. Or it may be a belief we've adopted because of the teachings of someone we admire and respect. It can also be acquiescence to a broader community sensibility. It's important when examining our beliefs to take it back to its initial planting because it is there we made the value decision that became our belief.

Let me share a story to help make that clearer.

Road trips are something I look forward to because I'll have uninterrupted time with some of my favorite thought leaders. Often that means listening to audio lessons from the late Jim Rohn, success mentor and philosopher.

I remember the first time I heard him speak about the importance of the origin of our beliefs. I was driving down to the Gulf Coast. I was going to spend the weekend with friends at their beach house, a much anticipated and needed respite.

The scenery was engaging, and the salt air still lingers in my memories of that day. But even with that anticipation and the seduction of sea and sand, Jim Rohn's words cut through, and I found myself stopping the car. I needed to hear again a statement he made. I wrote it down just to engrave the words in my mind. The essence of his teaching was this: *Every belief we hold must be the product of our own conclusion.*

Those are seemingly obvious words when you think about it, just a comment within his teaching. But it stopped me (and my car!) in my tracks. I recognized that I was making decisions in my life specifically about my work based on beliefs that were not in fact the product of my own conclusion. Giving myself permission to examine and even change some of those beliefs garnered significant change in life.

Can you think of any beliefs you have that you just accepted without any deliberation?

Beliefs are a key point when we talk about resilience. If we BELIEVE there are possibilities, we will act toward them. If we BELIEVE there are other perspectives that will allow those possibilities to emerge, we will seek them. You cannot be resilient and be closed in your belief. Our belief system must be alive and growing, a living part of who we are.

Our need to understand will then drive us to continuous learning. The sustained value of our belief system depends on new knowledge, new understanding to mature and flourish.

How do you know if you have too much, or if you don't have enough information? Ask yourself the following: Is it distorting, distracting, and even shielding my view? Or, is it expanding my line of sight?

In that same teaching I've referenced, Jim Rohn championed the idea of being a student of many, a follower of none. I adopted that as a guiding tenet in my life. I invite you to consider adopting it as well.

Named by *Time* magazine as one of the 100 most influential people of the 20th century, Sir Edmund Hillary had this offering on the subject after being one of the first to reach the summit of Mount Everest: "It is not the mountain we conquer, but ourselves."

Chapter 4

Perspective vs. Pain: Gratitude Above All Else

*N*othing challenges our response to life like pain. Whether physical, mental, emotional, or spiritual, when pain strikes, all bets are off when it comes to what we might have expected in our responses. That is why it's crucial for us to have a tool to create context and perspective for those moments. That tool is gratitude.

The Roman philosopher Cicero offered: "Gratitude is not only the greatest of virtues, but the parent of all the others."

But let's face it. It's hard to find gratitude when your world seems to be crumbling. And it's maddening when others tell you about that silver lining in your cloud, or that there's a purpose to everything. We know that. But at that moment, that's not what we need to hear. What we feel in that moment is not purpose; it is pain.

The most important thing we can do is to shrink the moment and gain some perspective, even distance from the pain. The fastest path to that distance is gratitude.

Why is gratitude so effective in times of pain? Because it flips over the emotions that typically come with pain. You cannot be stressed and genuinely grateful at the same time. You cannot be angry and grateful at the same time. They are counterintuitive emotions.

Here is the reality of this lesson. This is not about being grateful for *the pain*. This is not about that at all. In fact, sometimes it's about being grateful for anything but the pain. Sometimes we need to rest the eyes of our souls for a moment. We need a life lens that takes away the harsh painful glare. Simple gratitude does that for us.

If we are not grateful, we will not see the point in creating good. That's what gratitude is about – finding the good. It may not be about everything in the moment, but it can be about something, even if it is about something that we cannot yet see.

During some dark days when it took all my strength just to get through the day, there was a little corner of light always there because of gratitude. It was my diversion from pain to peace. Even if just for a moment, it immersed me in something outside of the pain.

Expressing gratitude for music, vision, the smell of fresh rain, finding joy in language, a child's laughter, and even a stranger's smile were all life vitamins of peace. Taking time to seek the good and be grateful begins to balance the scales.

During these days, I began a life practice that still sustains me now, and that is my gratitude journal. Each day I express gratitude in written form. Writing is a way of solidifying our thoughts and making them last. A journal is a natural expression for me as a writer. It can take many forms, but once we develop this life practice of expressing gratitude daily, the action becomes a native part of us, and something very special begins to happen.

It is important though that we also address the role of gratitude within each experience. Ultimately, that is how we evolve. Gratitude is possible even as we look at what initially is painful, if we allow ourselves to find it. And we need to find it because it is a pivotal fact that from gratitude, energy is created.

One of my mentors, David Bayer speaks about this in his program, *Mind Hack*:

> "In our everyday experiences, the problem is never the problem. The problem is the meaning that we give the experience we are having. Successful individuals have developed a habit of finding the gratitude and, in doing so, reshape their moment-by-moment experiences and position themselves in a state of high energy and, therefore, mental activity."

With a lens of gratitude, we begin to seek the good. We search for those reminders, and we find them. After all, whatever it is we seek, that is what we find.

Everything that happens makes something else possible. Everything. It is up to us whether what is made possible enhances our view and value in the world or diminishes it. By starting from a place of gratitude, we ensure our line of vision. We change how we see things so that what we see can change.

Having the privilege of raising my daughter and seeing her bloom into the woman she has become is something for which I am grateful. When facing my empty nest, focusing on my gratitude instead of on any void or loss changed the view. Being grateful for the relationship we enjoy and witnessing the many miracles in her life made those times even sweeter. That gratitude also led me to ask in grace what was made possible for the next season in my life.

It was without question a tougher scenario to find gratitude when my career was disrupted. But it was imperative I get there because all the possibilities for my future were found in leveraging all the good of what had brought me to that moment. I found my gratitude in relationships, resources, even learned resilience over the years.

Being grateful for my journey and where I am now positions me to build on that for what is next.

One of my favorite poems is Cavafy's "Ithaca." I revisit it each year in my personal reflections of the time now passed and the promise of what lies ahead. Within the lines of that poem are words that are very special in that they will always take us to that special place of grace and gratitude. You can substitute what you are grieving for the first word and find the power of the sentiment:

"Ithaca gave you the marvelous journey. Without her you would have not set out. She has nothing left to give you now."

The experiences I have been sharing here as a sort of touchstone for us in our conversation all had at their core lessons on gratitude. Even the one least likely. My health.

This is where I learned to divert my eyes from the pain to find other places for grace until I could see more clearly. I had to find gratitude first and then later connect it to the challenge. To begin the day being grateful for life is different from requiring ourselves to begin the day being grateful for the pain. If that is where we must begin, that is where we begin. Ultimately though, we will find our way to acknowledging grace within the pain.

Where did I find gratitude facing Hepatitis C? I found it in recognizing all the people whose lives championed mine. I found it in seeing all the things in life I never would have appreciated without going through that valley. I found it in the deepening of my faith and prayer life that continues to bring me my greatest peace.

The point is that we find what we seek. In gratitude, we seek the good. Nothing more powerful.

Chapter 5

The Path to Empowerment: Our Choices Live in Our Actions

We are not empowered by our thoughts. Not really. We are enlightened by them, even driven by them, but our true source of power comes when we are in action. I thought about writing this book a great deal. But it didn't create energy or become a reality until I begin putting words on paper.

Think about this for a moment in your own life. What do you think about doing? Are you trapped in thought? Or do you move into action? When you think about making healthier choices, do you move into that lifestyle?

A friend and fellow life coach recently reminded me that our true choices live in our actions. We think that we must first figure out our choices, but the reality is that the best ones find us based on what we set in motion. This is part of the miracle of the Law of Attraction.

Our resiliency muscle emerges as we begin to CREATE, when we MOVE thoughtfully into what is next.

When we take the first tentative steps on a path that opens for us, it can be daunting. It's not the path we had planned. But it is still our path to take, and as we take those steps and go around new corners, we begin to see opportunities that would never have been visible except for that breakaway from the path we had been on.

Consider this thought from Tom Bilyeu, co-founder of Quest Nutrition:

"Nothing carries a higher price than inaction. Nothing. If you let your life course be determined more by the moves you don't make, you will NEVER get where you want to go."

If you find that you (like me) sometimes hesitate when it comes to taking those steps, here are four lessons from my own reflections to consider.

Fear Holds Us Back

My first lesson was that the greatest thief of action is not what I thought it was. Have you ever thought of yourself or someone else as being a procrastinator? That was what I always thought was my main block to action. But procrastination at its core is nothing more than fear.

If we are not moving into action, we are held back by some form of fear. And sometimes, action is the only anecdote. Not words, not advice, not study, not even prayer. Sometimes it takes the action itself to dissipate the fear.

Eleanor Roosevelt said it beautifully: "You gain strength, courage, and confidence by every experience in which you really stop to look fear in the face. You are able to say to yourself, 'I lived through this horror. I can take the next thing that comes along.'"

Blame Keeps Us Stuck

The second lesson and action thief for me was blame. Sometimes we cannot move forward into action simply because we are stuck in the moment out of a sense of betrayal, even anger. Including at times, self-blame. An error in judgment, unintended or even intended but still regretted because of harm to another, can paralyze us.

The only anecdote for blame is forgiveness. Outside of gratitude, forgiveness is the most empowering response to allow ourselves to move forward.

Everything Changes

The third lesson is from the late Dr. Wayne Dyer. One of his core teachings was this: "When you change the way you look at things, the things you look at change." When you see events from a different vantage point, you see them differently, and you see everything around them differently. That new perspective will open pathways to action. The resiliency question "What does this make possible?" becomes more than a mantra. It's a way of living.

Live Your Values

The final and fourth lesson is that everything begins and ends with our values in life. We cannot live a life of value unless we first decide what value we want to live. That is our true foundation. Whatever we set out to do in our lives, the fundamental purpose will be found in our values.

To live a completely resilient life means that we take everything in and see it as a new possibility for achieving what is most important to us. The value we give the experience is directly related to how it aligns and supports our own values. Our values are what will show us the next action and then the next. They are the compass that never fails.

This, more than anything, is what acts as our focusing mechanism. How everything serves our core values becomes the beacon that lights our path, directs our steps, and shows us the way.

Our foundation is ready. We are prepared. Let's sail.

This is Harder Than I Thought: Change Is Not for the Faint of Heart!

*"With everything that has happened to you,
you can either feel sorry for yourself or
treat what has happened as a gift."*

*"Everything is either an opportunity to grow
or an obstacle to keep you from
growing. You get to choose."*
~WAYNE DYER

Change is not equal. It's not. A new highway goes in and provides us with easier access to the other side of town. That's change. We could see it as progress because it will save us time.

But to some, that change represents loss.

The loss of property to create the space for the highway would make that change have a different context. For some families, the addition of a higher tax to pay for its construction could be a significant financial burden.

The loss of trees and other environmental factors could impact the quality of the very air we breathe.

Change is not equal. Once all is said and done, our perspective of change is going to be directly related to its personal impact in our lives.

There are times when we believe we are ready for change, and we are not. There are times when we believe change is about loss, and it is not. There are many facets to consider when we talk about change. What it is and what it isn't. And the answers can and will change with every incident of change.

What we must fundamentally understand is that change will be as transforming as we allow it to be and in whatever way we choose for it to be. The responsibility of determining what it means lies within us.

We all aspire to something. Even if we haven't translated it into a specific goal, there is something we want more of, something we want less of, or something we want to be different. It is the ultimate dichotomy of our humanness. We resist change, yet it is change that we want more than anything.

The underlying conflict in this dichotomy seems to be that we want the change *we* want and nothing else. We do not want to have to put change to work; we only want change that works for us. But the best change quite often masquerades as something else, something perhaps we don't recognize for its true potential.

That's the essence of resilience, and why it must be our foundation before true change can happen. Being resilient means recognizing the opportunity in whatever comes our way. Once we've made the decision about what we want, then everything gets put to work to accomplish that. It's one of the principal lessons in Napoleon Hill's work, *Think and Grow Rich*. The decision or resolve begins everything. Without that moment, there is no touchstone.

This is where once again values and beliefs are paramount. By starting from a foundation of values, we can choose the meaning of any change based on how it will serve those values within our choices. But it is not for the faint of heart because when change is about who we are in the world, it can rock the very pins of that foundation.

It may not be easy, but it will be worth it as expressed by these words from Mark Twain:

> "Twenty years from now you will be more disappointed by the things you didn't do than by the ones you did do. So throw off the bowlines. Sail away from the safe harbor. Catch the trade winds in your sails. Explore. Dream. Discover."

Chapter 6

Whatever Happens, Happens to All of Us: Why Aren't We Ready?

Our life experiences are as unique as our fingerprints. But the essence of them is far more universal than we may think. I'm sure you have heard it said before: We are more alike than we are different. Events in our lives are also more alike than they are different.

History shows that things tend to move in cycles. We experience it year after year with the seasons. We *know* that things are going to change, and yet, we are surprised when they do. More importantly, for some reason we are not prepared.

When our children are born, we *know* that they are not going to live with us forever. We know that. We even go to great lengths to prepare them for a future where we will not be there to take care of them. All too often, though, we fail to prepare ourselves. Our complete focus is on their readiness.

And then we are surprised at the depth of the void left behind when they leave the nest.

We *know* that industries and markets change. We do. After all, we are consumers as much as anything else. There is no doubt that today we are choosing and buying differently than even a short time ago. We have evidence in our lives every single day that business and businesses are changing.

Yet, we fail to consider the impacts of that within our companies and our careers. The writing is truly on the wall. But because we wear blinders, we are blind-sided by the impact of those changes within our work. And when it comes to change, when your work is your world, it carries an even deeper devastation.

Let's face it, we *know* about aging and have for a while. We experienced it as observers of our grandparents and now our parents. We've even had those mornings ourselves where it's just a bit more challenging to hit the ground running. We have lain exhausted on the field of life far earlier than we would have expected.

Even with that knowledge, all too often we fail to seek out what we need to be doing to maintain the energy, flexibility, and good health required to live our fullest lives. We look up one day and face the dreaded thought that we are now the ones who are aging. The truth is, we've been aging from the time we were born. But at some point, we stopped paying attention to that progression or somehow expected it to not happen to us.

When my daughter was expecting her first child, I bought a book for her that has become a staple now for first time parents about what to expect during pregnancy. Then there are follow-ups about what to expect in the first year, the toddler years, and so forth.

We know that as our children progress chronologically, there are changes that we can anticipate. We begin to expect certain things to happen at certain times. Remember the excitement of the first time they sat without you holding them up? Or they got their first tooth? Took that first step?

Remember the chairs in grade school? We were expected to outgrow those chairs. It would be quite uncomfortable for a teenager to go through the day sitting at the desk they sat at in their early years of school. And have you ever met a child who doesn't tell you their age in increments? They are not just 4; they are 4 ½! As children, and even as parents, we looked forward to and celebrated every milestone, every new chair.

When do we stop doing that? Let's admit it. There is a point where we do. We stop seeing learning as something we should continue doing. We stop thinking about change as growth. We stop seeing our evolution as a celebration and start seeing it as something else.

We knew all along what was going to happen. We simply didn't prepare ourselves because as much as we know about what is going to happen, there is far more that we don't know, and that brings fear and uncertainty. We postpone facing that fear for however long we can, and therein lies the challenge.

Recognizing that is the first step to opening the door to resilience as we move through life's seasons. Once we learn to replace fear with the anticipation we once enjoyed, the battle is nearly won.

Chapter 7

Permission to Grow: Start at the Beginning, Start with You

I remember the early days of my newly emptied nest. My thoughts were constantly with my daughter. What was she doing? Did she have everything she needed? How could I help her adjust to her new life? These are all normal concerns for a parent to think about.

What is the problem with this type of thinking? The true underlying questions were not about her at all. They were about me and my role in life. What was I going to do now? Who would need me? How could I adjust to MY new life?

Those questions were harder.

I was unprepared. My world changed with that wedding on every level.

That's when I first began to acutely recognize the difference between *who I am* and *what I do* in life. Our roles continuously change. Another critical realization was that I could never give her the support she needed to grow if I was not giving myself permission to do the same. We never stop teaching our children by our example.

It always starts with us. We must take responsibility for ourselves before we take on someone else's needs or any situation.

Tyler Stenson is a songwriter and musician. He wrote and recorded a song used in a commercial that caught my attention. The music on that commercial was his song *We Grow*. There's a very special story behind the message of the piece. A main lyric reads: "We are entitled to change because we grow."

The backstory is what makes this song so relevant to resilience and growth. Tyler had done some recordings and built a following of fans. Tyler's work evolved because he grew as a person and as a musician. Some of those fans were unhappy about the changes.

They wanted the *old* Tyler back.

The song was Tyler's manifesto statement and response. He was entitled to change because he grew.

We all are entitled to the same privilege.

Tyler's song became a favorite and a bit of an anthem for me.

With his permission (www.tylerstenson.com), here is an excerpt of his work:

I heard you say that you wish I stayed
An older version of me — long before my change.
But, if we're not growing we are staying the same,
So I will welcome the change and stretch myself day
to day.
We're entitled to change because we grow.

If a seed can grow into a tree
And if that tree can grow leaves,
I ask, how is that different than me?
Because we both breathe and we come from the dirt
And that's where we will return
When both of our seasons fade.
We're entitled to change because we grow.

As we grow, so will the opportunities for us and the ways we express ourselves. But it starts with giving ourselves permission to grow.

When we give ourselves permission to grow, we allow new perspectives to come into view. And with those perspectives come magnificent possibilities we would have missed.

The most remarkable part? Whatever permissions we give ourselves serendipitously we end up giving to those we love and honor as well. They become an integral part of the legacy we leave because it is a part of the legacy we live.

Chapter 8

The Law of Reciprocity: Give What You Need

One of life's fundamental tenets is the law of reciprocity. This basically tells us that whatever we need is what we should give. If we need love, give love. If we need encouragement, give encouragement. It is as ancient as any truth we have. Even the Golden Rule supports this. Treat others as you want to be treated. What you want—even need—to receive is what you should give. Be the first to give.

This can be hard to understand. It can seem a bit selfish to give to others based on our own need. But when we give with pure intention, joy is the energy that surrounds us, and those around us begin to respond to our joy.

How do we do it? By determining what we need and finding a way to fill that need for others. If we are lonely, rather than focus on our loneliness, we can recognize that we are not, in fact, alone and can actively look for opportunities to fill that void in others.

The words of the always-wise Zig Ziglar, one of my father's heroes, come to mind: "You can have everything in life you want, if you will just help other people get what they want."

Whatever you need, champion that for others. Be the first to give what you need. It works. Before you know it, you will be championed by others as well.

There are many stories about the dividends of giving. The kindness of strangers is something we all celebrate and appreciate. What we may fail to recognize is that we play a role in those stories every day. We choose how we are going to show up in the world in every interaction we have.

Reciprocity is also a universal concept in this case.

It is not about getting back what you give. It is about giving from a place of grace knowing that grace will be there for you when that is what you need.

One of my favorite ideas around this is thinking in terms of a chain reaction, a domino effect. It's not a new concept, but for a very long time, unless we were talking about a game of dominoes, it wasn't something we intentionally set out to create.

And yet today we do.

Whether it's paying it forward at a Starbucks window, taking on an ice water bucket challenge in support of ALS awareness, or inviting friends and families to create gratitude posts on social media, as a society we are actively looking for ways to join with a cause and make our world a better place.

What is creating this force of good? From what I have observed, it stems from three fundamental shifts that have impacted all of us. First is the increased recognition that regardless of how different we may be, as a human race we universally share the same hopes and dreams, and yes, even fears. Technology has created more than a global economy. It has also created a global neighborhood. Instead of being limited to watching life go by from our front porches, we are seeing it from the pages and screens of social media platforms and digital communities. This brings us together in ways we might never have imagined and allows us to appeal to each other's basic humanity in ways we would never have dreamed possible.

The second part of this is that we're able to readily see and share what happens when we take those steps to join in. That serves to fuel the fire for more good. Imagine that if you just paid it forward at the Starbucks window and never found out you were number 498 in an ultimate line of over 700, as happened in St. Petersburg, Florida, you would still take satisfaction from having contributed to that one person. But now you can know that you didn't just impact one person, you were part of a movement in a single day that touched over 700 lives. That can be some heady and *hearty* stuff. It also means that the next time you pull up, you might even be number one in an ultimate line of over 700, instead of number 498. We like being a part of good things.

The third component of this is that it gives legs to our hope that there is good in our world. The news is filled with so much heartache. We need to know about that, too, because we are a part of that as well. But when we have the chance to catch sight of that flame of hope for the good in all of us, it is rejuvenating. We can pause amidst the clutter and chaos, and take in a moment that is just about doing some good. Those moments can even serve to stop the chain reaction of some of the heartache.

How incredibly powerful it is to know that we can create good with such simple acts, not just in the moment but within the moments to come, as our actions and examples create the genesis of so many more. Reciprocity is generated when each person who witnesses a kindness is inspired to create one of their own. In the end, the world is a better place—all because someone cared enough to drop the first domino.

That's what happens when we first look to what we can give.

"Since you get more joy out of giving joy to others you should put a good deal of thought into the happiness that you are able to give."   ~Eleanor Roosevelt

Chapter 9

What Does It All Mean?
Whatever You Decide

*W*hatever it is we encounter in life, the value of it is whatever we choose it to be. Triggered emotions are natural responses. The key is recognizing they are also *choices*.

Think about a specific challenge you are facing and ask yourself the following questions:

- Why does this matter?
- How is this helpful?
- What makes this hard?
- What am I grateful for in this situation?
- What does this make possible?

Our attitude toward change shows up long before our specific response. In almost all cases, to at least some degree, that attitude is dictating the outcome. Even as we are happy for someone else, we can experience a very different response for ourselves.

I recently read that our attitude acts like the advance person of our true selves. In other words, it shows up before we do, long before the main event. Over time, it becomes almost instinctive.

The question then is whether we have an attitude about changes in our roles and responsibilities that is pre-empting our personal growth and success.

If so, how do we change that?

We change our attitude by changing our perspective. That can begin with how we speak about it. Going through those questions can help. The real key though lies in the last question.

- What new people can I meet and serve?
- What new places can I experience?
- What new skills can I acquire and master?
- What new ideas can this generate?
- How does this expand the possibilities for my life and work?
- In summary, what does this make possible?

Our life seasons also contribute to our response in terms of our development and our wisdom acquired from experience. We are refining our philosophies along the way and becoming increasingly aware of our value and influence in the world.

We thrive when we keep our designer mindset open. There are always new and exciting factors coming in as those that have finished are moving out, even if only figuratively.

Our children growing up, heading to college, moving away, getting married. It doesn't matter who you are. This can be a very unsettling time. Our whole lives can seem to shift. No matter how much we're celebrating; within that change, there can still be a sense of loss.

I call it the nest dynamic: Relationships – Responsibilities – Resources

In my own life, I see this clearly in hindsight (that rearview mirror!) There is a relationship dynamic that shifts. Our children are always our children, no matter how old they are. But they become someone else as well. They become another adult and, in some ways, a peer. That relationship can bring a very different energy.

When we think about responsibilities, quite often we're really talking about purpose. We're so used to living our own lives at every level based on being responsible for our family's lives. When that responsibility shifts, it can bring with it a loss of purpose. What will we do with ourselves?

And those resources! Our time, money, and energy. When the priorities begin to shift, we often fail to recognize that how we leverage these resources also needs to shift.

It is here where we begin to learn and embrace the POWER of Permission, Perspective, and Possibilities.

Every change is an ending and a beginning. Every time our life progresses to a new season, it brings the ending of something we know so that we can replace it with possibilities that were not there before.

Think about this in terms of our calendar seasons. We can't have winter and summer at the same time in the same place. There are things unique to each of them. It is the same in our lives.

We may not want a season to end. But to get through to the point of permission, perspective, and possibility, we first must allow ourselves to grieve for what is left behind. How we do that is as individual as our fingerprints. But it is essential. And it starts, as always, with gratitude that it was ours to experience.

The key question is always this: What does this make possible? That is the essence of resilience and how we move with grace to what we create next in and with our lives.

What Do You Mean I Can't Stay Here? Opportunities in Rejection

"In the long run, we shape our lives and we shape ourselves.
The process never ends until we die.
And the choices we make are ultimately
our own responsibility."
~ ELEANOR ROOSEVELT

"It is always your next move."
~ NAPOLEON HILL

It was January 20, 2009.

My division's senior executive and I stood at the front of the room and faced our corporate staff. We had been through some challenging weeks due to layoffs across the country.

People were understandably nervous about the meeting and their jobs. But his message was clear: No more layoffs.

The relief was palpable. I remember feeling a tremendous reprieve myself that I would not have to face anyone else with those wrenching words: "Your services are no longer required." We could now start to rebuild.

When I arrived at the office the next morning, I called my own staff meeting with my direct reports and began mapping out our next steps. When my boss arrived, he stopped by my office. His request for me to meet him in his office felt normal—a routine request.

But when I arrived, his office door was closed. That was the first sign that something wasn't business as usual. I wondered who was with him but still did not feel any concern. After a few minutes, his assistant said for me to go into the office.

He was not at his desk. He was at a small conference table and with him was the head of the Human Resources department. My immediate thought was that we had a problem stemming from the layoffs. But I was wrong.

When your boss does not speak, when his eyes will not meet yours, it's a clear sign that you aren't going to like what the other person is about to say. I cannot remember the exact words that were ultimately said, but the message came through clearly. My services were no longer required.

I was stunned.

I had been a part of the start-up management team. Over the past decade, I had given blood, sweat, and tears to be a part of something we were all very proud to have built. I remembered the telephone conversation with the original founder when we named the company. I remembered the first time we broke $1M in sales and then $100M in sales. I remembered it all.

But on that day, in that room, I was the only one who remembered. The other two people present hadn't been there for those moments. They just remembered they had a job to do that morning, and that job was to relieve me of my duties. Because I was an executive, it was immediate. That meant security gathering my personal things from my office and escorting me to my car.

It felt like I had been punched in my gut. I could not speak, think, or move. I sat in my car and tried to remember how to operate it. I put my head down on the steering wheel and tried to determine what I was supposed to do.

I wanted to call someone and tell them what had happened to me. The startling truth was that every single person in my life that would even begin to understand my devastation was still in the building from which I had just been escorted. I felt completely adrift and alone.

Eventually, my senses (and sense) returned, and I navigated my way home. Over the next couple of days as I mulled over my options, I found myself reading some books that were part of my personal things at the office. One of them fell open to a page that held this quote from Earl Nightingale: "We become what we think about."

The quote caught my attention because I was in a *becoming* state, and my thoughts were all over the place. But I was also captivated by the name Earl Nightingale. I knew it was familiar but unsure why.

Then I remembered stories my dad had shared with me about Earl Nightingale's radio show back in the 1950s.

Although my dad wasn't alive to speak to me in person, he came back full force into my mind and heart through that book. I did some research and found that I could order digital copies of the recordings of Earl Nightingale's work.

I listened intently to that wonderful gravelly voice that had also encouraged my father all those years ago, and I eventually found my way to Nightingale-Conant where the course of my future started to become clearer. I engaged an extraordinary life coach and reclaimed my professional footing. I also regained a personal perspective that had eroded over time. The same thought leader that inspired my Dad a lifetime ago was now serving me.

What are you most afraid of losing? What feels like it would be the worst thing that could happen to you? I can tell you that, at that point in my life, it was exactly what had happened—losing my job.

Something happens when the worst thing you think can happen is what happens to you. You realize it's not the worst thing. In fact, when we practice resilience, we have the power to CREATE GOOD things from that rock bottom place where we find ourselves.

Over the next two years, my life would dramatically change. I started my own company, completed a new college degree, became certified as an Executive Life Coach, and created a life that integrated my personal and professional vision and purpose. At the time of this writing, it's now been eight years, and my life is unrecognizable compared to what it was before. It has been a journey to joy.

Was it difficult? Yes. Was it what I planned? Certainly not! My plan had been to focus on building someone else's company – not to launch my own! Would I have done this on my own without being fired? Perhaps in time, but certainly not when it happened.

This matters a great deal because my story is not a Cinderella story. I was happy before. I was accomplished before. I was successful before. But something happened. Through resilience, I had to find a new way to be happy, accomplished, and successful. And I did.

Chapter 10

We Are Not Our Work, Are We?
Finding Better Questions

*M*any of us, busy raising families, growing our careers, and living our lives, lose sight along the way of who we are and what we want. Our early dreams fade as we assume growing responsibilities. We begin to think in terms of leaving a legacy versus living one.

We focus on preparing for being "gone" with things like insurance, investments, properties, and a will explaining our wishes to our loved ones about what they should do when faced with closing out our lives once we're gone. We lose sight of the spirit of life. It's not about what we leave. It's about what we live. It's about our time. Our energy. Our love. The essence of us, not the ashes of us.

I remember shopping one day and seeing a plaque that had these words inscribed: "Find something you're willing to die for and then live for it." I found that thought compelling. I realized beyond my family and faith, I had no idea what I cared about at that level.

I needed to find out.

Defining success on my own terms became an excavation process. Have you ever watched a documentary that shows an archeological dig? You must carefully go through many layers, sifting and combing through years of silt and soil to get to the treasures. To find the story of the life that was there takes time, but it's essential if we want to get it right.

To get back to who I am and what matters to me, I had to sift through years of the story that up until then was my life. My core values emerged from that process much like the treasures on those archeological digs.

We can't build a life of joy if we don't know what joy is for us. In the words of Kevin Ngo: "If you don't make the time to work on creating the life you want, you're eventually going to be forced to spend a LOT of time dealing with a life you don't want."

I realized it was time to get clear about what I wanted and get busy creating a life that delivered that result. While that sounds wonderful as a sound bite, it was not easy.

If you've been at this place where your entire identity seems to shift without warning, you will recognize this crossroads.

I really had lost sight of what I wanted. I had to begin again, but this time, I was not starting from scratch. Now I could draw from the experience and wisdom in my toolbox that hadn't been there before.

I started crafting a personal manifesto that was completely energizing. It was also quite terrifying. I wanted to create my own life, but I was afraid of what I might lose in the process.

It was an opportunity I was excited about, but it also overwhelmed me.

When we start to carve out the life we want, all the changes that whirl around us become less like debris and more like a smorgasbord. We get to choose what works for us. Not once, not twice, but all the time. Which is a huge opportunity that also includes a significant amount of risk.

I began immersing myself in more introspective writings and works. I was brought back to a favorite poet, Rainer Maria Rilke. In his work, *Letters to a Young Poet*, he offered this sage advice:

> "I beg you to have patience with everything unresolved in your heart and try to love the questions themselves, as if they were locked rooms or books written in a very foreign language. Don't search for the answers, which could not be given to you now, because you would not be able to live them. And the point is to live everything. Live the question now. Perhaps then, someday far in the future, you will gradually without even noticing it, live your way into the answer."

It was clear I would need a new direction in my work. I discovered that, moving forward, how I chose to use my gifts and talents would only be limited by my vision for them. They could find a new home. I was no longer my work, and my work was not me.

When we are faced with change in our work, there are three plausible options for us.

Pause

This can be very powerful. Pausing. I believe in that. And it was my initial response. There are times when we need to take stock. We don't suspend our lives. They don't stop. But we do create space for reflection.

During the pause is when we explore without any restriction. It's not that we aren't occupied or productive—we are. But we're occupied in a way that isn't based on a long-term commitment, and we are mentally free to examine new possibilities.

Pivot

This is where we essentially continue doing the same work we have been doing, but in a slightly different direction. This can be an excellent option when you have skills with merit and worth in multiple arenas. This can be a progressive option once we are ready to move forward. The only requirement is that we see market value of our talents and skills versus just their employed value.

Propel

For many of us, fear has been a companion for some time, and we have held on to false security. When that rug gets more than a tug and we're on the floor, the risks are rearranged, and we are now ready to leap.

You may notice that none of these options involves holding on or bouncing back. Those were not considerations for me and may not be for you when it comes to your work. Key point: We cannot bounce back to a place that no longer exists.

Holding on to false hope is futile. Stagnation is the enemy. We pause to consider, pivot to continue, and propel to create. Each of us moves through these tiers at our own pace, but when we are committed to making a difference, not moving is not on the options list.

Let's talk for a moment about how this type of change may play out. Some people seem to just instinctively know what they want to do next. They have a very clear vision for their lives; resilience is alive and well.

There are others, though, who have no notion of what they want. All too often, they settle into a life that may be less than fulfilling and does not challenge them beyond whatever level they find themselves. Because they were unprepared and had no real skill in resilience, they became and remain in danger of staying adrift.

There is another group of people that are personally driven, but without a clear notion of what is next. Especially if they (we!) thought they were in the first group and now must face the reality that what they wanted is off the board.

There can be twists and turns that are less about direction than they are challenges for greater depth and meaning. No matter how developed your resilience muscle may be, it can appear on the surface not to be as progressive in terms of aspiration.

The journey can be more circuitous than one that is a steep arc of momentum.

In every case, we must learn to bring our best selves to the flow of the river of life and look forward to its current as it takes us to what is next rather than needing to always plot it out.

We must allow ourselves, as Albert Einstein taught, to look for what *is* rather than what we think should be. We must pursue true value over rungs of the ladder.

We must be willing to move beyond who we think we should be to become all we can be.

Chapter 11

The Surprises in Store: Dealing with Disappointment

When we think about resilience, we also need to consider where the roadblocks will be. In some cases, they will live in our assumptions and beliefs about people and relationships.

One of my favorite movies is *Nothing in Common* with Jackie Gleason and Tom Hanks. The film is both heartbreaking and heartwarming, often in the same scene. Tom Hanks' character is the son, an aspiring professional whose life has been disrupted by his parents' (Jackie Gleason is his father) separation. The disruption is both emotional and physical as the son must step in and help a father who rarely did that for him.

There is a moment near the end of the movie played out in a hospital corridor that sums up the heart of the story. The father has undergone surgery and has been released to go home. The son is pushing him in a wheelchair as they leave. The son is stunned and gratified when his father tells him that he was the last person he ever thought would come through for him. It is a beautiful moment on very human terms.

Expectations and assumptions. Who will come through for us? There will be surprises on both sides. The disappointments, though, are challenging.

If you have had a similar experience to mine where you unexpectedly lost your leadership position in your work, then you are nodding your head about now. You may find that the people you thought would be loyal to the ends of the earth were in fact only loyal to the end of the job.

It's a hard pill to swallow. Calls and emails are not returned. People are so BUSY! The exchanges are rushed and uncomfortable. The aftermath can feel like a masquerade ball where in the middle of the party, all the masks fall off and you find you've been dancing with a stranger and ignoring a friend.

While it is natural to feel disillusioned—even hurt—when relationships fail us, it is imperative not to dwell there. If we stay within the negative emotion, we will not be able to move forward. But those emotions can be very hard to release. Knowing how to release unhealthy emotion is a foundational skill within resilience.

Sometimes we feel justified in our feelings without even recognizing their cost. If we think of our personal perspectives as the window through which we see everything in our world, it can get easier to see how hanging on is distorting our view.

Imagine that window to the world. Now imagine that every feeling of anger, guilt, hurt, or resentment is like being in a car that is driving through mud puddles that splash onto the windshield. At first, you can barely see, but eventually the water evaporates, and you're just left with the debris. Some of it will blow away but what remains creates blind spots all over the windshield. Those blind spots are going to keep you from seeing everything you need to see to navigate through what's next.

Have you ever noticed that we struggle to let go most often when it means we're going to need to forgive ourselves or others? If you are facing this, here are some steps that will help.

Make peace with the past. We cannot limit our future based on our past. Cynicism does not serve us well. Our past is meant to prepare us for the future, not predict it. We must make peace with what has happened. The steps for that can vary, but in the end, we achieve a state of grace through forgiveness of ourselves and others so that we can live from a place of gratitude.

Be honest about the present and take responsibility for it. Personal responsibility is a significant factor for personal growth. Whenever we play the blame game, we are imprisoning ourselves as victims. We live "at the mercy" of circumstances or other people. Once we are honest about where we are and take responsibility for our life and everything in it, we are empowering ourselves to change it.

Let go of your excuses. I admire people that don't stop at one discovery. We've all heard the story of Thomas Edison's 1,000 tries to make a successful light bulb. He didn't make excuses about what didn't work; he just moved on to the next effort. But throughout those 999 previous attempts, other innovations emerged that we still use today. They may not have been the star he was seeking, but their value was evident. For 389 of them, he applied for and received patents.

Chemist George Washington Carver discovered over 325 uses for the peanut. His perspective? "Ninety-nine percent of all failures come from people who have a habit of making excuses."

Throughout our lives, we are going to be surprised by others and ourselves. From a place of resilience, it is impossible to fixate there. We move past those surprises or build upon them. What does this make possible?

Chapter 12

Back to the Basics: The Value of Life Practices

There is something comforting in routine, in the familiar. It keeps us from feeling completely adrift at a time when direction may not be clear.

When we have incorporated healthy practices into our lives that are constants, they become the familiar touchstones for our day, and they can keep us in motion.

We are drawn to them in times of confusion and uncertainty, but we develop them through daily practice.

An essential principal within resiliency is staying in action. Even if we pause in some areas for reflection, our overall life continues to move, and we must move with it. That is where having optimal life practices and honoring them no matter what is happening around us can be beneficial.

When I look back at where I may have faltered or struggled with staying motivated, in almost every case one or more of my own life practices had lost focus. Bringing them back into my routines inevitably supported getting my thoughts and direction back as well.

There are many reasons why this is so important, but chief among them is that when we are in crisis mode, we can also experience decision fatigue. We are facing monumental changes, and it can be overwhelming. When we have practices that are just part of our daily routines and rituals, they create a haven for us. They keep a thread of normalcy in our day, and they create outlets for releasing our thoughts and emotions in a healthy and constructive way.

Here are five practices that I invite you to consider adopting (and adapting) as your own.

The first is a <u>writing practice</u>. This is not about being an author or writer. This can take on many forms, but having a daily routine where you have self-expression is empowering and centering.

As it is for many, for myself this is my practice of journaling. My morning begins with my thoughts for the day, and my evening wraps up with my gratitude from the day. You can also do this via digital writing or audio recording. The key is daily self-expression.

Why journal? There are many reasons it can be valuable. First, the transfer of thought to paper via your own hand can be a powerfully affirming exercise. It can also be a form of release. In the case of a themed journal like my gratitude journal, it is a daily re-centering but also a resource for those times when I may be struggling. I can go back to those journals and experience anew all the things that touched me and moved my spirit.

The second and third practices focus on health and physical well-being. It is essential for us, particularly in times of stress, to maintain <u>proactive self-care</u> that covers movement and nutrition. A <u>movement practice</u> can be stretching, walking, a workout, or a myriad of other options. Just incorporate an activity that meets your own needs best.

Sometimes it can be fun to alternate your personal practice here, but the point is to regularly devote time to your physical body. Remember that this is part of a routine that's going to generate power in your day. When we are moving physically, we naturally move mentally, emotionally, and spiritually.

In times of stress, it is in our diets that we falter. But as Mother Teresa taught us: "If you want the lamp to keep burning, you must put oil in it."

We need the best oil for the best light. After all, it is much harder to think well, do well, and live well if you don't feel well. Set yourself up for success with healthy practices.

The fourth practice is a <u>spiritual practice</u>. This can be reading, listening to music, meditation, prayer, or any combination of these activities. Recognize that this is a personal space but extremely important. We were created as a multidimensional being: body, mind, AND spirit. We must care for each of those dimensions.

The fifth practice is less specific and yet perhaps the most life changing. It is this: <u>Strive to make a difference every day</u>.

The idea of legacy often emerges in discussions about changes in the seasons of life. For what do we want to be remembered?

We often see people taking on causes and engaging more in their communities when going through personal change. That's a wonderful strategy, but this point is more about what we do every day.

Make it a life practice to make a difference for someone every day.

In the words of Anne Frank: "How wonderful it is that nobody need wait a single moment before starting to improve the world."

Why focus here daily? Because whether we recognize it or not, we have an impact every day in every encounter. Sometimes good, sometimes perhaps not, but we have a choice. If we set an intention every day of making a positive difference in our world, the dividends we achieve in life satisfaction are priceless.

One of my favorite thoughts on this comes from Ralph Waldo Emerson. He shared this wisdom: "It is one of the most beautiful compensations in life that no man can sincerely try to help another without helping himself."

Use these five life practices to create a life system that will guide you through from now to next. Not once – but every time throughout your life.

Chapter 13

The Miracle of Learning: The True Root of Resilience

Resiliency takes courage. We must be willing to face a situation fully open to the possibilities it brings. That can go beyond being daunting and at times be close to terrifying.

What gives us that kind of courage?

It is knowing that whatever is there for us, it is something we can do if we choose to do it. In the words of Henry Ford: "Whether you think you can or you think you can't, you're right."

What is really at the core of thinking that we can? It's simple: We already have! We have accomplishments in our lives. We have learned new things. We have mastered new skills. With each of those milestones, we built our resiliency muscle. Because we have, we know that we can.

Some of my favorite moments with my daughter and now my granddaughters have been seeing their faces light up and declaring, "I did it!" Whether it's tying their shoes, riding a bike on their own for the first time without training wheels or mastering the cartwheel! Can you feel that emotion just thinking about that image? You did it! We believe we can because we have.

Accomplishment is the only source for true confidence. That confidence also feeds our sense of self and self-worth. When we are worthy, it extends to the idea that we are worth the effort.

Because resiliency rarely leads us down a path of ease, it's important to have a reason to travel there. It goes beyond hope or faith in what lies ahead. It speaks to what lies within and our self-worth. We feed that sense of worth by ever expanding and growing our view of ourselves and our place in our world.

That's the real miracle of learning—not the knowledge itself—but the realization that there is no limit to what we can do because there is no limit to what we can *learn* to do.

With each opportunity to grow our resiliency muscle, we learn more about our response triggers and coping mechanisms. We learn how to think broader and deeper. We learn how to challenge our perspectives and demand more of ourselves and our experiences in life. We learn.

It stands to reason that if learning were such a critical part of building resiliency, we would give it priority and create strategies around it. Part of being prepared is thinking about the possibilities of what could happen. Everything. The good and the bad. This isn't meant to dissuade or discourage us. On the contrary, when we are prepared it allows us to move through whatever may happen. We have anticipated and provisioned for all the possibilities from the onset. We can close any gaps through strategic learning.

What life skills do we need to have?

What knowledge would be valuable?

As we close those gaps, our confidence rises, and our fears diminish.

Let's talk for a moment about balance. When we consider balance, we tend to think in terms of our life and work, but in truth, it matters within each part of our lives.

For example, we need a balanced approach to health as well as to our financial profile. Our personal network should be diversified and expose us to perspectives with range and depth.

The same is true for learning. We need to have core skill building for our professional endeavors and soft skill development overall. We also need to integrate things into the mix that are perhaps outside our standard fare and develop creative interests as well as skill.

This is an area where quite frankly I have not always had the right mix. My professional development always took precedence over my personal development. I considered learning a part of my work, not necessarily my life. A cooking class might have been fun, but who had the time? I certainly didn't. I learned that we must *make* the time.

I made a conscience decision to begin incorporating some creativity into my learning mix. Where did I start? A pottery class! Why pottery? Because I love that art form, and it seemed like something that would completely occupy my attention.

That was, after all, part of the point. I wanted and needed a complete departure from business as usual.

I also felt that it would introduce me into a world of artists where I could absorb some of that creative energy. I also thought it might be fun to play in some mud! And it has been.

My very first pottery piece was a small dish with a bird perched on its edge. It became a Mother's Day gift for my Mom. Now a grandmother myself, it had understandably been a long time since my gift to her was something made by my own hand. It felt good to do that again, and it gave the present a richer meaning for her as well.

What lessons in resilience did I take from this learning experience? Some thoughts well beyond the art form itself:

- When we are willing to become a beginner at something, we renew our true love of learning.
- Even the simplest of materials have the potential to create beauty.
- To make things happen, we are going to need to be willing to take some risks and get our hands dirty (sometimes literally).
- Pressure and heat create strength and transformation.
- We all sign our work in one way or another.

Helen Keller once said: "Life is a great adventure, or it's nothing."

Learning is the greatest adventure of all.

Chapter 14

It Takes a Village – But Which One? The Power of Community

I am the oldest of five children. It's never been easy for me to let someone else call the shots. Some call it being a natural born leader. My brothers and sister would just say I'm bossy. There's probably truth in both responses.

One of the most challenging things for me when my job ended was knowing how to be in a place with seemingly nothing or no one to lead. I had focused everything on one role in my life. That role had me front and center all the time. Then, suddenly I wasn't. It felt daunting to think about rebuilding my place in the world.

We like our comfort zones, and quite often that includes keeping people close by that add to our comfort. I am not a natural networker. I soon realized, however, that there is a difference between networking as a verb, and building and nurturing a network as an asset.

Our best associations with people will include an alignment of values. There it is again – the importance of knowing our beliefs and values. For me, it became the most natural way to reconnect in my new world. What changes do you want to be part of? What problems do you want to address? Who else shares that commitment? Those associations are priceless and beyond measure because of the impact you will achieve together.

We will naturally find kindred spirits on this path. Some are just ahead of us, and some may be coming along side. But there is a kinship that is natural because of who we are versus just what we do professionally. When I want feedback on something now, I can tap into some brilliant perspectives that take me in directions I would never find on my own. And I can do the same for them.

It has been said by numerous thought leaders that we are the average of the core group we spend the most time with in any given area of our life. If that is the case, why not make those relationships intentional? Why not look at the area of our life where we know we need growth, and focus first on how our relationships are a part of creating those possibilities?

The first step is just being honest with yourself about your relationships. Then look at the core areas of your life. Which areas are your focus?

If health is a critical focus and goal for you and no one in your inner circle represents the standard you want to achieve, it's time to make some changes. That doesn't mean you end friendships. It means you intentionally seek out people who are going to share that goal with you.

Over time, this method may result in the waning of some relationships because of your own investments of time, but in the end, it could also mean that you begin to have a positive influence on those friends. They could also begin to champion those goals for themselves.

That brings us to our second step. We must examine this same perspective about our contribution back to our circle.

I recently heard about an interesting practice one married couple uses in this area that is insightful. They check-in with each other every week by asking this question: "On a scale of 1 to 10, 1 being very disappointed and 10 being completely happy, how would you rate our relationship?"

Some weeks the answer is 10, and some weeks it isn't. There's a follow-up question, though, that is the changemaker. If the answer is less than 10, the question becomes "What would it take to make that a 10 for you?"

We can't hold people (or ourselves) accountable within a relationship to do something when they don't know what is needed. What a great practice!

The third step is having actions aligned with our intentions. Simply put, if it's not on your calendar, it's not important to you.

Let your calendar become your measurement of your relationship intentions and attentions. Those calendar entries should not just be about time together. They should also be actions we take on each other's behalf. Give priority to your promises and your people.

Kathi C. Laughman

Our circle is not only about where we are today. We are not meant to stay where we are. We are meant to grow. Our circle is the looking glass to our future.

One of my personal favorites as a thought leader on this subject is the late Charlie Tremendous Jones. He taught that where we are in five years is going to be determined by the books we read and the people we meet.

Our best village will bring influence and imagination while providing us the opportunity to return the same in kind.

There Must Be Some Mistake: When It Happens to You

"When it is dark enough,
you can see the stars."
~ RALPH WALDO EMERSON

I was traveling to Portland, Oregon, for a conference. I boarded the plane, found my seat, stored my luggage, and sat down. To my horror, the seatbelt would not reach across my lap to fasten. My weight had ballooned, and the bubble of denial was bursting. My battle with weight had been on-going for over ten years. I continued to gain weight with no explanation.

To say I was mortified would be an understatement. The cabin attendant on that flight wasn't having a great day herself, and customer service for the fat gal in row 30 wasn't in the cards. The irony is that I don't know of any moment in my life that I felt that small.

I vowed on that flight that when I got home, this was going to end—whatever it took. I even called from Portland and made a doctor's appointment.

There are moments in our lives that are marked and unforgettable. We can always go right back to that place and remember every detail. Such was the day of that appointment for me.

It started out with excited anticipation. I was doing something. I just knew I was going to conquer this once and for all. This doctor was going to be the one who would champion my cause, get to the source, and tell me how to fix it. But that excitement quickly turned to icy fear.

I clearly remember sitting in the examination room, wearing one of those lovely gowns we get to wear for these excursions, thinking about the appointments I had that afternoon. They would all be cancelled, but I didn't know that then.

The doctor was taking a bit longer than normal, and I was beginning to wonder if they remembered I was still there, waiting to get my results. Finally, the doctor returned.

Her first words were these: "What do you know about Hepatitis C?"

A low hum started in my ear. What on earth was she talking about? What in the world was Hepatitis C? I was about to find out.

I had decisions to make, but I wasn't ready to make them. I didn't know enough to feel comfortable about making choices regarding treatments or even doctors. I took all the information and made a follow-up appointment with the recommended specialist.

I took what I knew and determined what I needed to know next. I then went into action to sufficiently close my knowledge gaps, so I could make an informed choice. Resilience. I didn't understand it at the time, but everything that had happened to me up to that point had conditioned me to move into action. It made all the difference.

I learned that the type of Hepatitis C I was dealing with was a tough one – highly resistant to treatment. I learned that many (read *most*) people either cannot finish the treatment or end up chronically ill, living in a continuous cycle of treatments, constantly battling the disease.

I also learned about a new treatment protocol that was very tough to take but was getting favorable results.

I learned all of this within 48 hours.

But here is what else I learned: For every statistic, there are at least two numbers; the percentage of those that don't get cured and the percentage of those that do.

We choose which side of the equation to focus on. To claim as our place.

I decided to focus on the percentage of those that were cured. I made an active choice, a committed decision to be in that group. And I set out to discover what that would take. And then that's what I did.

In the beginning, I could not even fathom the level of perseverance that would be required, but my resolve was strong.

My story is not heroic by any stretch of the imagination. It's not even complex at the end of the day. It was closing my knowledge gaps and taking the necessary actions before and during treatment that made it possible to persevere and find the good.

These words from Sir Winston Churchill often came to mind: "It's not enough that we do our best; sometimes we have to do what's required."

Chapter 15

Worry Is a Waste of a Good Imagination: What Is True?

*H*ave you noticed that the unknown is where we experience the most fear?

We are afraid of what will happen because we don't know what will happen. Those cords of control fray because when we don't know, we go into overdrive to know, even when it means wasting our imagination with worry.

There is a valid argument for wanting to know. After all, when we know we can be more confident in our response. We have more assurance that we really are making things better (versus worse).

We should seek to know. But that is different from the idea that we *must* know. There will always be something, even many things, that we don't know. In other words, no matter how much we know, we'll never know what we don't know.

Worry is wasted because it never results in anything more than speculation. It is a waste of our imagination.

There is empowerment in that acknowledgement because it gives us permission to move on without having to know everything. It also helps us grow and brings us the capacity we need to deal with guilt or even regret.

We do the best we can with the information we have at the time. Acknowledging the limits of current knowledge also allows us to revisit decisions and adjust them as new information becomes available.

When we allow imagination to fill in what doesn't yet need to be filled in, we begin to project scenarios not even likely. What if? It's no longer a statement about possibility. What if we try this or that? It becomes a threat. What if the worst happens? What if I lose everything? What if?

The dream turns to a nightmare with the twist of the lens on the kaleidoscope, and monsters appear.

I have played out entire scenarios in my head just knowing the worst is about to happen; and then I realize how ridiculous it is. I don't have any reason to believe the worst just because I don't know what is next. It's where the mind can be our greatest battlefield. When we are afraid, and something is beyond our control, it can push us to desperation.

How do we combat this? How do we come to the place where worry is replaced with patience and peace? This is another fundamental learned response within our resiliency practice. How do you respond before you know what will happen?

The answer is far simpler than you think. The answer is this: You don't.

It comes down to three basic things. First is that we start with what we know. Second is that we determine where critical gaps exist to make an informed decision. And then we move into action where we can.

What do we know? Sometimes it is far more than we think and sometimes far less. To stay in a perpetual state of resiliency, our perceived knowledge requires continuous testing. What was true yesterday may not be true today. New information comes to light and changes our interpretation of what we previously thought were facts. Probing for validation is vital for leading us to gaps we need to close.

The source of information is also a factor. We have access to what I call information infinity. That can be in our favor, and it can work against us because it plants seeds of misinformation when the sources themselves are not legitimate. When time is a factor in our decision process, vetting our sources is our first point of business.

Ultimately, we must choose the information we are going to use to make as informed a decision as we can. This is true in any situation where stakes are high. What do you know? How true do you believe your information is? What sources are available to both confirm and provide useful knowledge?

The action, more than anything, is going to prove the information based on the results we get. We can then adjust as needed. By moving into action and examining actual results, we don't leave any room for wasted worry. We are occupied with meaningful work.

Know what you know. Know who knows what else you need to know. Assemble your knowledge, and make your decision. Then act. Then measure. And repeat the cycle.

We will never have a foolproof way of making the right choice every time. But by following this pattern, we have the absolute opportunity to make our choices right every time.

As St. Francis of Assisi said: "Start by doing what's necessary; then do what's possible; and suddenly you're doing the impossible."

Chapter 16

There Is No Competition in Grief: Lessons in Compassion

What has happened to you? Where is your grief? Odds are that you have experienced it. Here is the next lesson I learned from my dance with Hepatitis C about resilience:

There is no competition in grief.

Over the course of the next ten months, I would spend time in clinics and doctors' offices. I would look around at my chair mates and wonder about their stories. What was their battle?

Those rooms tended to be quiet. I wanted, sometimes even needed, conversation. Sometimes someone else wanted that as well. Creating a relief valve with laughter was miraculous in those rooms. In those rooms, solace was found in the fact that our battles were shared.

I learned that there is an incredibly fine line between believing your grief is more and berating yourself into thinking that your grief is less than anyone else's. It isn't either of those. It's your grief. This is sacred ground. There is no competition.

The true balm was finding compassion for myself and for others. Finding it first for others enabled me to claim it more readily for myself. We grieved together. We also celebrated together.

There was no resentment when someone came out with a smile. To the contrary. There was hope. Every smile brought hope that the next smile walking out could be ours. And eventually it was.

I was reminded that true listening is an art form.

There is a public service video series that was produced some time ago by the Cleveland Clinic. When I saw the first video it seemed to just show people in the halls, elevators, and rooms of a hospital. It was however in fact the beginning of what would become a series of videos focused on finding compassion through empathy.

The theme is driven from a quote by Henry David Thoreau: "Could a greater miracle take place than for us to look through each other's eyes for an instant?"

The scenes take us through the hospital but with the added captions of circumstances and thoughts for the people in the video. A normal day at the hospital. But everyone there had their own grief and story.

A young girl bringing the family pet to visit her dad for possibly the last time.

A woman staring blankly into space trying to comprehend what she's been told.

A man being wheeled in and dreading the appointment, fearing he has left it too long.

A woman drinking coffee while her son is upstairs on life support.

A man sitting in his room thinking about his daughter's wedding he will miss.

There is no competition in grief. Only compassion. Those stories were there even when we didn't know them.

In the end, the video asks us to examine how we would treat them if we knew. If we could see through their eyes, hear what they hear, and feel what they feel. Would we treat them differently?

You cannot feel sorry for yourself for very long when you shift to a compassionate view of others. As you focus on them and give them what is needed, as we've already discovered, it's given to you in return tenfold.

And this is where I ultimately found gratitude for my Hepatitis C. This level of compassion is not anything I could have achieved without that experience. That kind of compassion is a gift. And its ripple effect is truly miraculous.

Chapter 17

Mind vs. Body: Understanding Energy as a Resource

*H*ave you ever read the back of a medicine bottle? I will confess that before my experience with Hepatitis C, that was not something I did with any real care. We certainly look at the dosage and consider interactions with other medicines, but what else? There is much in the fine print we skim past. Frankly, we depend on doctors, nurses, and pharmacists to not let us make mistakes.

The specific treatment protocol I chose had three different drugs. Each of them had a distinct purpose, and each carried their own risk. Each one also had their own list of possible side effects. Not only was the information there for me to see, I was also told about what could happen by my medical team.

As someone who had taken very little medication and rarely had any issues with them when I did, I will admit that I was not concerned. It turned out to be a case of denial, thinking I would somehow be immune. It was one place where in hindsight I know I could have paid more attention. The list of *possible side effects* would later become the checklist of my *actual side effects* experience.

Although they were all challenging, even debilitating at times, one of the side effects that was the most difficult for me was loss of energy. I was not prepared to abruptly lose the ability to do anything—and without warning—often for long stretches of time.

Imagine that every day you left home with your errands list in hand and the gas gauge on your car did not work. You don't know how much fuel you really have, and you have no idea when it will be depleted. Wherever it ends, your day ends. No warning, no way to know. You can't just push the pedal harder for gas to flow. It won't. It is gone.

That was my new reality. This was not a matter of pushing through; there wasn't anything in reserve to use to push. The frustration was enormous.

Before tackling this illness, I would work myself into a state of exhaustion and then work some more. Provided my mind was going, my body just had to cooperate. But in this case, the body always won. There was nothing to do other than what my body demanded.

Stop. Rest. Recover. My appreciation for energy was forever changed.

What happens when you don't know when you are going to have to stop? You listen to your body. Then, you get highly protective of your energy resources and give priority to what matters most each day.

Doing what mattered first became my focus, perhaps even my obsession.

It was my goal to make sure that my daily practices allowed me to get maximum value from every moment. I paid attention to my body and the signals it was sending. Rest became a demand, no longer a luxury.

The shifts in how I came to value time and energy would become the foundation for how I lived going forward, well beyond healing. Using the power of discipline and intentional daily practices is what enabled me to not just endure the treatment, but to win the battle. It was clear to me that this was the true power in any race to the finish line.

What we do each day to make certain that we are doing what matters most is ultimately what creates our future success. That concept became the basis for my life mantra:

Live today like you want tomorrow to be. Live well.

Chapter 18

Adjusting the Sails: Progress Over Perfection

*G*oing back and reading my journals during this time is like reading an extended essay on being patient with results and impatient with action. That fundamental truth became another element in my strategy shifts for life.

Each day I did what I could. The sails were constantly adjusting. A new drug reaction or side effect would have to be managed. Energy levels were erratic. The doctors could not tell me anything definitive about a timeline.

It was markedly different from anything I had experienced.

Here's the goal: Healing.

Here's the plan: We're going to try this and see if it works.

Conversations about what we would do if it didn't work were just squashed. We would talk about that when and if that time came. There was no time or energy expended on anything other than the next step.

Progress.

There is no motivation in the world more powerful than progress. It doesn't matter what you are doing or why you are doing it. Progress is what will ultimately keep you in the race.

Even the most miniscule movement will work, but you must see some progress. That is why measurements mean so much.

Overall, I did not enjoy my very frequent lab visits. In fact, they were some of the hardest days. But without them, this journey would have been very different. With each milestone test, I found the strength to get to the next milestone.

The distance between the diagnosis and the finish line was too great. I had to have some markers in between to keep me going. The staff at the clinic became members of Team Kathi, and they knew it. We celebrated each good result and worked together when they were less than what we wanted.

I will never forget my final check-in with the lab. We were in tears, and we were celebrating! That celebration could only happen because we bonded over each milestone along the way. We became collaborators in my healing.

The key is to know what markers matter and have a way to measure them. Then adjust as you go.

Adjusting the sails. Progress over perfection.

As Sir Winston Churchill said:

"Every day you may make progress. Every step may be fruitful. Yet there will stretch out before you an ever-lengthening, ever-ascending, ever-improving path. You know you will never get to the end of the journey. But this, so far from discouraging, only adds to the joy and glory of the climb."

Wherever You Are, You Aren't Staying There: A New Lens for Change

*"You can do anything you decide to do.
You can act to change and control your life.
The process is its own reward."*
~AMELIA EARHART

Change is inevitable. The question is who decides what is changing and how is it changing. We have far more influence in our lives than we might expect.

The first step is acknowledging that fact. Understanding you are not going to stay where you are. Knowing you are going to be moving.

That single shift held significant transformation for me. It's not that I don't embrace change—I do. I've always been growing and moving, but I began to recognize that I limited that growth to safe channels.

To be a master practitioner of resilience, we must be willing to leave any of our swim lanes and gain a new perspective. We must embrace risk as well as change. We must learn to be comfortable with discomfort.

When something happens (changes) that affects your self-confidence, it is easy to slide into a pattern of fear that will make you unsure about every decision.

Is this the right thing to do now? What if this isn't the best choice? What if this doesn't work?

On the surface, this can feel like every previous decision you made was wrong. But that's not valid. I did fine. You have as well. We didn't get where we ended up from failure. We got there from life. And wherever we find ourselves, this is clear and always true:

It's not where we will stay.

No matter what we are facing, the most important gift we can give ourselves and those we care about is to simply begin weighing our options, and making decisions that are followed by action.

"Don't dwell on what went wrong. Instead, focus on what to do next. Spend your energies on moving forward toward finding the answer." ~ Denis Waitley

We must take responsibility for what is next. Surprises are detours, not cancellations. That is how we continue to grow our resiliency muscle and master its miracles.

Eleanor Roosevelt said: "You gain strength, courage, and confidence by every experience in which you stop to look fear in the face. You must do the thing you think you cannot do."

Chapter 19

A Fairy Tale Life?
Once Upon a Time Is Here and Now

When a story begins with the words *Once upon a time*, we expect to hear a fairy tale. One of those stories where everything is extraordinary, and the ending has everyone living happily ever after. I happen to believe in those fairy tales, or at least what they represent.

Somehow, over the course of time, we stopped remembering the middle of the story. All we remembered was *Once upon a time* and *happily ever after*.

When life didn't work out that way, we stopped believing in the fairy tale. We stopped trying for the happy ending. We lost the brilliance of resilience.

The middle of the story is where we learned about courage, perseverance, and doing the right thing even when it was the hard thing to do. We learned that happy endings come at a price, that there is sacrifice in getting there.

What if once upon a time could really be here and now? What if happily ever after was not just for children's stories? What if we could lay claim to that?

I believe we can. Here's the catch: We will need to put the middle of the story back in. We will need to develop our story, make the sacrifices, and slay our dragons. In other words, do the work. Resilience is the work. Instead of resisting the work, we need to cherish it. Only resilience can make the fairy tale come true.

For many years, any time I was asked to name my top five goals in life, one thing that was always on my list was to write a book. It was my *Once upon a time* story. Unfortunately, it stayed in fairy tale land for me. Why? Because I wasn't doing the work. I had the desire but not the commitment. I wasn't willing to make the sacrifices I needed to make, but that changed. Largely because of the life events I've shared with you here.

Those disruptions created space in my life, and I started to do the work. I signed up for writing workshops, participated in writers' conferences, and started looking (and hiring) coaches and mentors who would be able to guide me down the path of becoming a published author. I went from talking about a book to writing a book.

What changed? It wasn't the desire. It wasn't even the skill, although that continues to be honed. Here's what changed: I picked up that sword from the fairy tale and started slaying the dragons blocking my path. I made the sacrifices. My schedule had to make room for this. The investments had to be made in time, money, energy, and effort to make the *happily ever after* my here and now.

What is it that you want for your life that has been in that secret place (or maybe not so secret a place) of your mind that is your fairy tale? Which life events have felt like setbacks for what you desired most? Where can you begin to put resilience to work in your life?

One of my mom's favorite television shows is *Dancing with the Stars*. She has loved dance since she was a young girl in the 1940s. We've all delighted with her in some of the triumphs and life stories in that show. One season, Sherry Shepard was a competitor. For some reason, she resonated with me more than any of the others. As she was departing from the competition, she offered this insight:

> "And, I wanna say, to every person out there—that thing that scares you the most, that makes you say, 'I don't know if I can do it, I'm scared,' run towards it because it's so amazing on the other side."

I agree. There is nothing like being on the other side of once upon a time. Here and now is unbelievably wonderful! Resiliency is our ticket there.

Chapter 20

The Practice of Resilience: Asking the Other Questions

*I*ntegrating resiliency in our life practices requires that for every question we ask, we must also ask what I call the "other questions."

What we are considering is the fundamental need to move beyond *positive* thinking to *possibility* thinking. We must be able to look at every side of our choices. There is always another question to consider. The other question is also what quite often delivers us the greater return. It is where resiliency lives.

A simple example of this might be reducing the clutter in our lives. We ask ourselves what we need to eliminate. This can be physical within our environment or more resource centric around our money, energy, and time.

It can seem counterintuitive to say that in our review and self-discussion, we also must ask ourselves what we need to add into our lives. As we've already seen, endings and beginnings are important to see together.

While it may seem that it doesn't matter which we ask first, it does. The better place to start is *what* is it time *to begin*? To add. Given the resources needed for that, *what* is it time *to release*? Where do we need to make room?

We essentially move into an exchange. That can be significant in how we perceive and handle the practice of letting go. In this case, what we thought was the primary question, in truth, is secondary although vital.

Questions that drive insight are the ones that move us forward. Here are three areas of questions to consider for developing a possibilitarian point of view that leads to resilience:

What is the real change I want to achieve?

Know your true objective or desired outcome from the change. Your *why*. Keep asking until you find it. You cannot stay on track if you don't know where you really want to go.

It starts with the question of why. *Why?* You continue to ask that question until you get to an emotion. Then you've arrived at what you really want to achieve.

Suppose your change is that you want to lose weight. *Why* do you want to lose weight? You might say that it's because you want to be healthier. *Why* do you want to be healthier? Perhaps you are thinking about your children or grandchildren. *Why* do you want to be healthy for them? It could be any number of answers, but for the question of why to be answered you are going to get to an emotion, and most likely, it's going to have some element of fear or loss. We counter that with actions we think will prevent it.

A shortcut for this exercise is this: Take a 3" x 5" index card, and on one side write down what it is you want to achieve. Think about it and fast forward in your mind to the time that it's done! You've achieved it! Savor that for a moment. Turn the card over, and on the other side write down how you feel now that you've achieved it.

Here's the insight: The real goal is found on the side where you wrote down what you will feel. That's really the change you want. The action is just what you've decided for now will give you that.

The more you practice this, the faster you will get to your core value. When we keep our core value at the forefront, resilience is a natural result because we are not looking at a circumstance without context. We are examining everything against how it can serve what we value.

What options am I avoiding?

This is crucial because, quite often, what we refuse to consider is our best option. We all have non-negotiable positions. That's not what this is about. This is about what we might be afraid to try, or think isn't even a possibility for us. It's about removing limitations, not compromising boundaries.

Within resilience, how we perceive things will change and what we never considered before can move front and center. This is not about avoiding something just because we may not want to do it, although that is part of it. It is also about avoiding something because it doesn't seem big enough or it's failed in the past. Any number of reasons can come into play.

What is important is that we exhaust every possibility without initially limiting ourselves to probabilities.

Quite often, this is where we may need to engage others to help us recognize what we might be avoiding. But to get you started, look for where you may be using terms such as "never" or "always." Those are danger signals that limited thinking is in play. We also need to test our assumptions. A simple question like *What assumptions have I made?* will begin to uncover other opportunities

If you consider that something is not an option, go back to your series of *why* questions until you get to the root of it. Your assumption may be valid, but chances are (good) that it's an outdated judgment that could be eliminated.

What am I missing?

What is going to trip us up? Where are the blind spots? What aren't we considering that needs to be addressed? What are the risks? If you know them, you can mitigate them from the start, or at a minimum, have a plan in place to address them should they happen.

If you do not know the risks, you have not fully defined what you want. If this is a challenging area for you, start with the assumptions you've already identified or identify them now. Your risks will be in your assumptions. What are you assuming to be true? What if it is not? What are you assuming is not true? What if it is?

As a gift, I received a very special stone from my iPEC family where I studied for my certification as an Executive Life

Coach. It stays with me as a kind of talisman when I'm thinking through something challenging.

On one side, the word 'problem' has been engraved. It literally covers the entire surface. On the other side is the word 'solution.' The solution resides within the problem itself. When we examine the problem from all sides, we will find the solution is there. The other question is what will take us there.

In one of President John F. Kennedy's speeches, he reminded us of the truth in this idea with an example from the Chinese language: "When written in Chinese, the word 'crisis' is composed of two characters – one represents danger and the other represents opportunity."

Chapter 21

A Spiritual Quest:
Seeing the Whole of Our
Personal Journey

For us to fully understand resiliency, we must first embrace why it even matters. It matters because we matter. This goes beyond our role now or in the future. It's higher than that. This is where spirituality comes into the equation. This isn't about religion, although religious practices may be part of it. I know many people who do not consider themselves religious but do ascribe to being highly spiritual.

Where religion and spirituality do meet is in their practice. Even if you are a religion of one, there will be some level of practice involved for it to be effectual in your life. This brings us back to the fundamental idea of values.

When I have sought to define the essence of spiritually, what I always come back to is this: Our spirituality is defined by what we value, what we seek.

What do you seek? I'm not talking about *things* here. What do you at your most vulnerable place seek? What is that? That's essentially a spiritual quest.

One of my favorite teachings from the Bible is about spiritual gifts. We often quote the ending of that discussion where it talks about love. But what we miss is that it's resolving a discussion about the hierarchy and value of talents and gifts.

The lesson is that it doesn't matter what you do or what your gift might be. What matters is why you do what you do. It comes down to only three things that matter: faith, hope, and love.

That's the whole of our life and our spiritual quest – seeking faith, hope and love, and living based on those qualities we seek as we develop our values around them. This is essential when we look at resiliency because more than anything else, these pull us through those times in life where we need wind for our sails.

Hope is such a powerful emotion. It's why we try. Faith is the fuel that keeps us trying even when it's not easy. Think about it. If you want someone to act, even yourself, find the hope. For us to act, we need to have sufficient hope that the outcome will be what we want.

Hope is the belief that something can be true. It is possible. It may not be probable, but it is possible. What we must realize is we want that assurance before we invest ourselves— before we do the work—because sometimes that work is daunting.

The greater the hope, the greater the chance will be that we will take the necessary steps and make the sacrifices. After all, there is a price for every promise.

There is more to the miracle of results, though. Because hope without faith is not enough. Hope is different from faith. The difference is subtle but important. It is in the combination that we find the magic, the miracle.

When we have hope, we believe it *can* happen. But when we have faith, we believe it *will* happen. That's true motivation. It goes beyond the initial leap. It is walking the tightrope of life knowing you are going to make it through.

That again brings us back to a spiritual quest at our core. Hope can help us take the first step, but only with faith will we be able to keep walking. I find that I'm not as careful with hope as I am with faith. Hope is easy. Faith takes work, but faith is where the promise comes true.

The more we follow this, the easier it gets to really believe and have faith in what we can do, in the difference we can make not just in our own lives but in the lives of others and ultimately in the world.

We matter. That's the love. It is worth holding on to hope and stepping out in faith because of who it's for. It's for us. It's for the promise of us. Resilience is worth it because we are worth it.

A life that creates, shares, grows, and is ultimately expressed by our values will produce a life that has those values as its outcome. It is only when we deviate from that guidance system that we falter.

In the words of Albert Einstein: "Strive not to be a success, but rather to be of value."

One of my favorite books that I revisit often comes from Mark Victor Hansen. I had the privilege of meeting him in person shortly after I read the book, and have him autograph my copy. I asked him if he would sign a specific page because of its special meaning to me. The book is *The Miracles in You.*[4] It is written as a series of twelve miracle scrolls. It was the fifth scroll that spoke to me. That scroll is this: "I Expect Miracles"

That scroll reminded me of the wisdom of Albert Einstein when he said: "There are only two ways to live your life. One is as though nothing is a miracle. The other is as though everything is a miracle."

When we begin with a life view that holds the core belief that miracles abound, I believe that is what we will experience.

---

4 Hanson, Mark Victor (2015). *The Miracles in You: Recognizing God's Amazing Work in Your and Through You.* Franklin, TN: Worthy Publishing.

Chapter 22

From Powerless Effort to
Effortless Power:
Living Your Legacy

How do we bring all this together? By looking at what we ultimately seek and the value of resilience in achieving it.

We all have an inherent need to know who we are and what we value. We all search for a purpose for our lives. We want to be engaged with work that means something to us and is creating a difference in the world.

Our personal power, our ability to create good from whatever life brings comes from our spirit, our faith, and our absolute commitment to those values.

To be resilient begins with knowing what we want tomorrow to be and then living today in a way that will deliver on that promise. Every single day. No matter what the day brings.

We must live today like we want tomorrow to be. To live in resilience is to live with that purpose always in mind.

My personal values have their origin in the experience of growing up in a nurturing environment steeped in love and high in expectation. By certain standards, it would have appeared that we were just an average family. We were certainly not rich financially. Yet, we did not live average lives and still don't. There was always an expectation (and example) to continuously grow into more as contributors in our community.

The legacies from the lives of the multiple generations that came before us instilled a love of family, compassion for others, and a sense of responsibility for living an honorable life.

My parents had a passion to grow in knowledge and service. I've recognized lately the genesis is here for why I am so driven to keep learning and growing. The distinction, though, and greatest gift from their example is that the learning is not just for the sake of accumulating knowledge. It is to be able to more effectively serve. I can honor their legacy by living my own.

We must understand *why* we do what we do; why we *think* the way we do; why we *respond* as we do. Because those are the questions we must keep asking ourselves to achieve the results we want and need.

My message is very simple. We each need to know who we want to be. That is the foundation of everything. What are the core values we want to serve? That is ultimately who we become. From there, we just need to keep our lives on a path that provides us with the opportunity to serve those values. It is a much clearer path than we might believe.

Resiliency cannot thrive without the foundation of values.

Who do we want to be, and is that who we are? If so, how do we put those values into service? If not, what steps do we need to take to grow into that person?

What knowledge and skills do we need to gain? What people do we need to surround ourselves with to grow into that person? The questions must be asked and answered all throughout our lives.

While success is empty without a purpose, true resilience isn't possible without it. That is what I've learned and lived and now share with you.

This is my vision for this work: To help you see that no matter where you are today there is more value in the rest of your story than you can possibly imagine. That to me is exciting news!

I am so blessed and grateful that my own great-grandparents, grandparents, and parents all did just that. They were always living forward. They enjoyed their moment in time and invested it in the future.

Each of us is a miracle. We come into this life with our own soul print, and we make a difference every day, even when we aren't conscious of it.

I love to share this story about my Dad. Although he took his last breath on earth in 1988, he remains a very strong influence and mentor in my life. That to me is the ultimate legacy – when our wisdom lives beyond us. I'd like to share that story with you.

In the 1950s, there were two men who worked in a factory in northern Ohio. One of them worked the afternoon shift and the other the night shift. They did not know each other. Yet their lives would intersect and create profound change.

The young man working the second shift had just finished his tour of duty as a Marine during the Korean War. He and his bride had moved from West Virginia to Ohio in search of better opportunities. In addition to his regular hours, he often worked the night shift for extra income.

One night he was doing just that when he was assigned to a machine next to the other man in our story. Bear in mind that this was not mentally taxing work. In fact, boredom was something they continuously contended with, each in their own way.

That night, over the humming of the machines, our young Marine heard a very distinctive voice talking about all his possibilities and how to reach the goals he had set for himself simply by changing his thoughts.

It was as if this man was speaking directly to him. Intrigued, he went in search of the source and found the other man listening to a portable radio. The man speaking on the radio was Earl Nightingale. It was a life-changing moment.

Immediately our young Marine was determined! To earn enough money to buy his own portable radio, he decided to take on an extra job instead of just extra shifts. He had discovered his mentor even before he knew what a mentor was, and he didn't want to miss a single opportunity to hear more! That encounter changed his life.

That extra job? It was working as an attendant and mechanic at a local gas station. What happened? Ultimately, he didn't just show up because he worked there as a mechanic. In time, he showed up because he owned the business. He listened. He learned. And then he moved into action.

If we asked, I doubt that the other man in the story would tell us that the most important thing he did that day was take his radio to work. He wouldn't say that he changed lives just listening to his radio. But for that young Marine, undoubtedly that was the case. It set his life on a different course. It did the same for mine. That young Marine was my Dad.

Throughout my life, what I learned most from him—beyond the values of faith and family—was the miracle of personal leadership and development.

He defied the odds. He surpassed every expectation.

He became a deeply spiritual man. He lived with a quiet grace and humility that remains a part of his legacy. There was never a time that he was not reading or, later, listening to recordings and tapes. In fact, I still have his books and some of those early recordings! From that night shift in the factory until his death, my Dad continued to live and celebrate learning and growth, each and every day.

My Dad. He never lost sight of who he was. He never lost his vision of who he could become. And he never stopped growing into that man. He lived his legacy every day of his life. Not without challenges. But always with purpose. With resilience. I am so honored to continue to shine a light on that path.

"Learn to enjoy every minute of your life. Be happy now. Don't wait for something outside of yourself to make you happy in the future. Think how precious is the time you spend, whether it's at work or with your family. Every minute should be enjoyed and savored."

~Earl Nightingale

Live today like you want tomorrow to be.

Live well.

A Gift for You

*T*hank you for reading this book.

These words from Theodore Parker have been cited by Abraham Lincoln and Martin Luther King, Jr. about what makes a book valuable:

> *"The books which help you most are those which make you think the most. The hardest way of learning is by easy reading: but a great book that comes from a great thinker – it is a ship of thought, deep freighted with truth and with beauty."*

Those are the books that we seek. Those that make us think. Those that inspire and incite us with the ideas shared in them.

At the start of our time together I shared with you that it was my desire that the lessons shared from this season of my life would speak in some way to your need and that you would walk away with a fresh perspective. My sincere wish for this work is that something on these pages has made you think, inspired you and incited you into action in your own life.

To help you in that quest, I invite you to continue our time together and join our circle. A special gift is waiting for you that will help you as you take your own steps forward into a life of meaning.

Join us here and receive your gift: http://www.mackenziecircle.com/adjusted-sails/

Acknowledgements

Almost every writer I know started their love affair with words as an avid reader. That was certainly the case for me. I remember being a young girl in elementary school and opening the pages of the first book that transported me into the world of story tellers.

That first book was *Sue Barton: Student Nurse* by Helen Dore Boylston. Each day after school I could be found at the library. I relished every word, every page through all seven books in the series. Even now, over five decades later there are scenes from those books I vividly remember. Some years ago, I was gifted a well-loved copy of the first book in that series. It is one of my most treasured possessions. The acknowledgment of those that made this book possible begins in that library in Northfield, Ohio.

For my own work as a writer there are many people that invested in bringing my work to life. While there are far too many to mention individually, a few of the key contributors are these:

Connie Ragen Greene was one of my earliest mentors and the first person to invite me to participate in a collaborative book. It was fortuitously on redefining and claiming success on our own terms. My thanks for the opportunity and yes, the book is still available on Amazon! Donna Kozik and Margo DeGange would later bring other opportunities and taught me a great deal about the publishing world.

My work as a writer has also been enriched by two incredible women in the on-line and magazine publishing field: Cathy Alessandra and Caterina Rando. It was my privilege to serve their communities as a contributing writer first for Cathy's magazine Today's Innovative Woman and later for Caterina as an online expert in her Thriving Women in Business Community.

Lynne Klippel has been another person of influence. Although a wonderful writer in her own right, she chose to focus her energies on bringing fresh voices to the world as an author's coach. She was my first writing coach and remains a friend. In the very beginning of our time together, she gave me a special pen to use at my first book signing event. A copy of this book was signed with that gift and sent to her with my deepest gratitude.

Of course, beyond the writing, this book would not be the work that it is without the influence of my own life coaches and mentors. Thank you Ann Babiarz, Kyle Wilson, Pamela Slim and Michelle Prince for your continued investment in the success of others.

Special acknowledgment is also due to fellow members of master mind groups that have been a part of my personal and professional journey. My life and work has been richly blessed by those friendships. I am particularly grateful to my accountability partners from those groups, Michele Laine and Karla Rose Hudson. You both have been an integral part of helping me go from *once upon a time* to *here and now* with this work.

To my friend and publicist Sandy Lawrence I say thank you from the bottom of my heart. You kept the flame alive more times than you could possibly know, and I love you for it.

Mention is also due my sister of the heart Carlon McGough who spent many hours listening and reading these words and helping me find my way back when I stumbled. No one has ever had a better friend and confidante.

To my children and grand-children I humbly offer these life lessons in the hope that they will live beyond the page in a special way for each of you. To my brother Roger, thank you for keeping my panic in check every time the computer and I tangled!

To my personal hero, our Super Sam: Thank you for inspiring me every day with your sweet spirit and generous heart.

And finally, none of this would matter at all except for my faith and God's love in my life. My story is His story. Every word is for His glory and written by His grace.

Live today like you want tomorrow to be. Live well!

Kathi

About the Author

*K*athi C. Laughman specializes in overcoming the unexpected and rescuing plans that have gone awry. With over twenty-five years of experience in business intelligence, she is a respected voice in executive leadership circles.

In 2009, Laughman founded The Mackenzie Circle LLC, a coaching and consultancy agency aimed at helping other leaders ask the right questions and teaching them to combine their business acumen and life intelligence for winning strategies in their life and work. She currently serves as President and Chief Possibility Partner of The Mackenzie Circle LLC, and she is an ICF-certified business strategist and executive coach.

In addition to her successful entrepreneurial career, Kathi is also an inspirational speaker, a best-selling author, and a member of the Forbes Coaches Council. She currently resides in Spring, Texas.

You can contact Kathi and learn more about her work at: www.mackenziecircle.com.

www.ingramcontent.com/pod-product-compliance
Lightning Source LLC
Chambersburg PA
CBHW071350090426
42738CB00012B/3073